The Bureau of Indian Affairs

KNOW YOUR GOVERNMENT

The Bureau of Indian Affairs

Frank W. Porter III

CHELSEA HOUSE PUBLISHERS

Chelsea House Publishers

Editor-in-Chief: Nancy Toff
Executive Editor: Remmel T. Nunn
Managing Editor: Karyn Gullen Browne
Copy Chief: Juliann Barbato
Picture Editor: Adrian G. Allen
Art Director: Giannella Garrett
Manufacturing Manager: Gerald Levine

Know Your Government

Senior Editor: Kathy Kuhtz

Staff for THE BUREAU OF INDIAN AFFAIRS

Associate Editor: Pierre Hauser
Copy Editor: Karen Hammonds
Deputy Copy Chief: Ellen Scordato
Editorial Assistant: Theodore Keyes
Picture Researcher: Patrick McCaffrey
Designer: Noreen M. Lamb
Production Coordinator: Joseph Romano

3 5 7 9 8 6 4 2

Library of Congress Cataloging in Publication Data

Porter, Frank W., 1947–
  The Bureau of Indian Affairs / Frank W. Porter III.
    p.   cm.—(Know your government)
  Bibliography: p.
  Includes index.
  Summary: Surveys the history of the Bureau of Indian Affairs describing its structure, current function, and influence on American society.
  ISBN 0-87754-828-5
      0-7910-0852-5 (pbk.)

  1. United States. Bureau of Indian Affairs—Juvenile literature.   2. Indians of North America—Government relations. [1. United States. Bureau of Indian Affairs. 2. Indians of North America—Government relations.] I. Title. II. Series: Know your government (New York, N.Y.)   87-30275
E93.P83 1988   CIP
353.0081'497—dc19   AC

CONTENTS

KNOW YOUR GOVERNMENT

CHELSEA HOUSE PUBLISHERS

Government:
Crises of
Confidence

Arthur M. Schlesinger, jr.

From the start, Americans have regarded their government with a mixture of reliance and mistrust. The men who founded the republic did not doubt the indispensability of government. "If men were angels," observed the 51st Federalist Paper, "no government would be necessary." But men are not angels. Because human beings are subject to wicked as well as to noble impulses, government was deemed essential to assure freedom and order.

At the same time, the American revolutionaries knew that government could also become a source of injury and oppression. The men who gathered in Philadelphia in 1787 to write the Constitution therefore had two purposes in mind. They wanted to establish a strong central authority and to limit that central authority's capacity to abuse its power.

To prevent the abuse of power, the Founding Fathers wrote two basic principles into the new Constitution. The principle of federalism divided power between the state governments and the central authority. The principle of the separation of powers subdivided the central authority itself into three branches—the executive, the legislative, and the judiciary—so that "each may be a check on the other." The *Know Your Government* series focuses on the major executive departments and agencies in these branches of the federal government.

The Constitution did not plan the executive branch in any detail. After vesting the executive power in the president, it assumed the existence of "executive departments" without specifying what these departments should be. Congress began defining their functions in 1789 by creating the Departments of State, Treasury, and War. The secretaries in charge of these departments made up President Washington's first cabinet. Congress also provided for a legal officer, and President Washington soon invited the attorney general, as he was called, to attend cabinet meetings. As need required, Congress created more executive departments.

Setting up the cabinet was only the first step in organizing the American state. With almost no guidance from the Constitution, President Washington, seconded by Alexander Hamilton, his brilliant secretary of the treasury, equipped the infant republic with a working administrative structure. The Federalists believed in both executive energy and executive accountability and set high standards for public appointments. The Jeffersonian opposition had less faith in strong government and preferred local government to the central authority. But when Jefferson himself became president in 1801, although he set out to change the direction of policy, he found no reason to alter the framework the Federalists had erected.

By 1801 there were about 3,000 federal civilian employees in a nation of a little more than 5 million people. Growth in territory and population steadily enlarged national responsibilities. Thirty years later, when Jackson was president, there were more than 11,000 government workers in a nation of 13 million. The federal establishment was increasing at a faster rate than the population.

Jackson's presidency brought significant changes in the federal service. He believed that the executive branch contained too many officials who saw their jobs as "species of property" and as "a means of promoting individual interest." Against the idea of a permanent service based on life tenure, Jackson argued for the periodic redistribution of federal offices, contending that this was the democratic way and that official duties could be made "so plain and simple that men of intelligence may readily qualify themselves for their performance." He called this policy rotation-in-office. His opponents called it the spoils system.

In fact, partisan legend exaggerated the extent of Jackson's removals. More than 80 percent of federal officeholders retained their jobs. Jackson discharged no larger a proportion of government workers than Jefferson had done a generation earlier. But the rise in these years of mass political parties gave federal patronage new importance as a means of building the party and of rewarding activists. Jackson's successors were less restrained in the distribution of spoils. As the federal establishment grew—to nearly 40,000 by 1861—the politicization of the public service excited increasing concern.

After the Civil War the spoils system became a major political issue. High-minded men condemned it as the root of all political evil. The spoilsmen, said the British commentator James Bryce, "have distorted and depraved the mechanism of politics." Patronage, by giving jobs to unqualified, incompetent, and dishonest persons, lowered the standards of public service and nourished corrupt political machines. Office-seekers pursued presidents and cabinet secretaries without mercy. "Patronage," said Ulysses S. Grant after his presidency, "is the bane of the presidential office." "Every time I appoint someone to office," said another political leader, "I make a hundred enemies and one ingrate." George William Curtis, the president of the National Civil Service Reform League, summed up the indictment. He said,

> The theory which perverts public trusts into party spoils, making public
> employment dependent upon personal favor and not on proved merit,
> necessarily ruins the self-respect of public employees, destroys the
> function of party in a republic, prostitutes elections into a desperate
> strife for personal profit, and degrades the national character by lower-
> ing the moral tone and standard of the country.

The object of civil service reform was to promote efficiency and honesty in the public service and to bring about the ethical regeneration of public life. Over bitter opposition from politicians, the reformers in 1883 passed the Pendleton Act, establishing a bipartisan Civil Service Commission, competitive examinations, and appointment on merit. The Pendleton Act also gave the president authority to extend by executive order the number of "classified" jobs—that is, jobs subject to the merit system. The act applied initially only to about 14,000 of the more than 100,000 federal positions. But by the end of the 19th century 40 percent of federal jobs had moved into the classified category.

Civil service reform was in part a response to the growing complexity of American life. As society grew more organized and problems more technical, official duties were no longer so plain and simple that any person of intelligence could perform them. In public service, as in other areas, the all-round man was yielding ground to the expert, the amateur to the professional. The excesses of the spoils system thus provoked the counter-ideal of scientific public administration, separate from politics and, as far as possible, insulated against it.

The cult of the expert, however, had its own excesses. The idea that administration could be divorced from policy was an illusion. And in the realm of policy, the expert, however much segregated from partisan politics, can never attain perfect objectivity. He remains the prisoner of his own set of values. It is these values rather than technical expertise that determine fundamental judgments of public policy. To turn over such judgments to experts, moreover, would be to abandon democracy itself; for in a democracy final decisions must be made by the people and their elected representatives. "The business of the expert," the British political scientist Harold Laski rightly said, "is to be on tap and not on top."

Politics, however, were deeply ingrained in American folkways. This meant intermittent tension between the presidential government, elected every four years by the people, and the permanent government, which saw presidents come and go while it went on forever. Sometimes the permanent government knew better than its political masters; sometimes it opposed or sabotaged valuable new initiatives. In the end a strong president with effective cabinet secretaries could make the permanent government responsive to presidential purpose, but it was often an exasperating struggle.

The struggle within the executive branch was less important, however, than the growing impatience with bureaucracy in society as a whole. The 20th century saw a considerable expansion of the federal establishment. The Great Depression and the New Deal led the national government to take on a variety of new responsibilities. The New Deal extended the federal regulatory apparatus. By 1940, in a nation of 130 million people, the number of federal workers for the first time passed the 1 million mark. The Second World War brought federal civilian employment to 3.8 million in 1945. With peace, the federal establishment declined to around 2 million by 1950. Then growth resumed, reaching 2.8 million by the 1980s.

The New Deal years saw rising criticism of "big government" and "bureaucracy." Businessmen resented federal regulation. Conservatives worried about the impact of paternalistic government on individual self-reliance, on community responsibility, and on economic and personal freedom. The nation in effect renewed the old debate between Hamilton and Jefferson in the early republic, although with an ironic exchange of positions. For the Hamiltonian constituency, the "rich and well-born," once the advocate of affirmative government, now condemned government intervention, while the Jeffersonian constituency, the plain people, once the advocate of a weak central government and of states' rights, now favored government intervention.

In the 1980s, with the presidency of Ronald Reagan, the debate has burst out with unusual intensity. According to conservatives, government intervention abridges liberty, stifles enterprise, and is inefficient, wasteful, and arbitrary. It disturbs the harmony of the self-adjusting market and creates worse troubles than it solves. Get government off our backs, according to the popular cliché, and our problems will solve themselves. When government is necessary, let it be at the local level, close to the people. Above all, stop the inexorable growth of the federal government.

In fact, for all the talk about the "swollen" and "bloated" bureaucracy, the federal establishment has not been growing as inexorably as many Americans seem to believe. In 1949, it consisted of 2.1 million people. Thirty years later, while the country had grown by 70 million, the federal force had grown only by 750,000. Federal workers were a smaller percentage of the population in 1985 than they were in 1955—or in 1940. The federal establishment, in short, has not kept pace with population growth. Moreover, national defense and the postal service account for 60 percent of federal employment.

Why then the widespread idea about the remorseless growth of government? It is partly because in the 1960s the national government assumed new and intrusive functions: affirmative action in civil rights, environmental protection, safety and health in the workplace, community organization, legal aid to the poor. Although this enlargement of the federal regulatory role was accompanied by marked growth in the size of government on all levels, the expansion has taken place primarily in state and local government. Whereas the federal force increased by only 27 percent in the 30 years after 1950, the state and local government force increased by an astonishing 212 percent.

Despite the statistics, the conviction flourishes in some minds that the national government is a steadily growing behemoth swallowing up the liberties of the people. The foes of Washington prefer local government, feeling it is closer to the people and therefore allegedly more responsive to popular needs. Obviously there is a great deal to be said for settling local questions locally. But local government is characteristically the government of the locally powerful. Historically, the way the locally powerless have won their human and constitutional rights has often been through appeal to the national government. The national government has vindicated racial justice against local bigotry, defended the Bill of Rights against local vigilantism, and protected natural resources against local greed. It has civilized industry and secured the rights of labor organizations. Had the states' rights creed prevailed, there would perhaps still be slavery in the United States.

The national authority, far from diminishing the individual, has given most Americans more personal dignity and liberty than ever before. The individual freedoms destroyed by the increase in national authority have been in the main

11

the freedom to deny black Americans their rights as citizens; the freedom to put small children to work in mills and immigrants in sweatshops; the freedom to pay starvation wages, require barbarous working hours, and permit squalid working conditions; the freedom to deceive in the sale of goods and securities; the freedom to pollute the environment—all freedoms that, one supposes, a civilized nation can readily do without.

"Statements are made," said President John F. Kennedy in 1963, "labelling the Federal Government an outsider, an intruder, an adversary. . . . The United States Government is not a stranger or not an enemy. It is the people of fifty states joining in a national effort. . . . Only a great national effort by a great people working together can explore the mysteries of space, harvest the products at the bottom of the ocean, and mobilize the human, natural, and material resources of our lands."

So an old debate continues. However, Americans are of two minds. When pollsters ask large, spacious questions—Do you think government has become too involved in your lives? Do you think government should stop regulating business?—a sizable majority opposes big government. But when asked specific questions about the practical work of government—Do you favor social security? unemployment compensation? Medicare? health and safety standards in factories? environmental protection? government guarantee of jobs for everyone seeking employment? price and wage controls when inflation threatens?—a sizable majority approves of intervention.

In general, Americans do not want less government. What they want is more efficient government. They want government to do a better job. For a time in the 1970s, with Vietnam and Watergate, Americans lost confidence in the national government. In 1964, more than three-quarters of those polled had thought the national government could be trusted to do right most of the time. By 1980 only one-quarter was prepared to offer such trust. But by 1984 trust in the federal government to manage national affairs had climbed back to 45 percent.

Bureaucracy is a term of abuse. But it is impossible to run any large organization, whether public or private, without a bureaucracy's division of labor and hierarchy of authority. And we live in a world of large organizations. Without bureaucracy modern society would collapse. The problem is not to abolish bureaucracy, but to make it flexible, efficient, and capable of innovation.

Two hundred years after the drafting of the Constitution, Americans still regard government with a mixture of reliance and mistrust—a good combination. Mistrust is the best way to keep government reliable. Informed criticism

12

is the means of correcting governmental inefficiency, incompetence, and arbitrariness; that is, of best enabling government to play its essential role. For without government, we cannot attain the goals of the Founding Fathers. Without an understanding of government, we cannot have the informed criticism that makes government do the job right. It is the duty of every American citizen to know our government—which is what this series is all about.

About half of America's 1.4 million Indians live on reservations in housing ranging from traditional adobe villages (top) to dreary modern subdivisions (bottom). Since the mid-1800s, the Bureau of Indian Affairs has managed the affairs of reservation Indians, trying—with limited success—to help them overcome chronic health and economic problems.

ONE

An Uneasy Intermediary

Until the 1950s, the Three Affiliated Tribes of Fort Berthold, North Dakota—the Hidatsa, the Arikara, and the Mandan—were among the most fortunate Indian groups in the United States. During the 1800s, while other tribes fell victim to the diseases of the white man or the brutality of the U.S. Army, the Fort Berthold Indians lived in peaceful isolation along the Missouri River. Whereas many tribes suffered the trauma of being forcibly relocated hundreds of miles from their ancestral homelands, the Fort Berthold Indians were given a reservation (an area of land reserved for use by Indians) where they had always lived. During the first part of the 20th century, they became largely self-sufficient, whereas many other tribes had to depend on federal assistance. In a picturesque valley along the Missouri, the three tribes built a community with schools, homes, a hospital, a sawmill, and acres of rich farmland.

But in 1956, the federal government decided to build a dam on the Fort Berthold reservation to generate electrical power. The dam created a huge lake that consumed 156,000 acres of the reservation and most of the Indians' homes and business enterprises. Tribe members were forced to relocate to new towns consisting of mobile homes and prefabricated units. As compensa-

15

tion, they were given $7 million in damages and $5 million to cover the cost of moving—even though the actual value of the land was probably around $100 million. "We gave up a whole way of life for the Garrison Dam," Alyce Spotted Bear, chairperson of the Fort Berthold tribal council, said several years later. "We may have been poor, but at least we were happy, at least we were self-sufficient and could get by without public assistance."

The decision to build the dam was made by Congress, which has power over federal Indian policy by virtue of a clause in the Constitution that states, "The Congress shall have power to regulate . . . commerce with Indian tribes." But the policy was implemented by a federal agency called the Bureau of Indian Affairs (BIA), which then, as now, had responsibility for managing the affairs of reservation Indians. Although the BIA ostensibly was (and is) dedicated to improving the welfare of Indians, in this case it did little to oppose a federal program that had a devastating effect on an Indian group. In fighting the plan for the dam, the Fort Berthold Indians had sought legal assistance from the bureau, but BIA attorneys were reluctant to put up resistance because it meant fighting their own employer, the government.

The Fort Berthold episode typifies the troubles Indians continue to have many decades after the federal government abandoned its policy of dealing with them by military means or through treaties. The incident also illustrates the troublesome nature of the BIA's position as an intermediary between Indians (including Alaskan natives—Eskimos and Aleuts) and the federal government.

The agency has fulfilled this role since 1824, when it was established by Secretary of War John C. Calhoun to execute Indian policy enacted by Congress. Since that time, several other agencies—including the Indian Health Service, the Department of Housing and Urban Development, and the Department of Justice—have joined the BIA in providing services for Indians. But the BIA continues to have primary responsibility for Indian affairs and is the only agency that deals with Indian tribes on a government-to-government basis.

In addition to acting as trustee for 53 million acres of Indian land, the BIA currently has numerous other duties. It is responsible for Indian education—operating 112 Indian schools, helping tribes to set up schools of their own, appropriating funds to public schools that Indian youths attend, and developing special vocational and adult education programs. The bureau also functions as a "government in miniature" on many reservations, providing services that non-Indian communities receive from local and state governments. These services include police protection, road maintenance and repair, welfare payments, and job training. But the bureau's most important function is to help

16

tribes take over management of their own affairs. The BIA encourages tribes to set up their own governments, assists them in starting business enterprises, and, when possible, transfers to them responsibility for providing services that the BIA usually supplies.

The BIA provides services only to Indians who belong to tribes officially recognized by the federal government. In 1987, there were 512 such tribes, whose members constituted about half of the total Indian population of 1.4 million. The population served by the BIA is a very diverse group. Most of the tribes have their own languages and distinctive customs, and about 300 of them have their own reservations.

The BIA's mission has changed several times during its history, in accordance with shifts in federal Indian policy. In the BIA's first years, when the goal

A Chippewa Indian attends a BIA-operated high school on a reservation in Montana. The BIA spends almost a third of its budget on education, operating 112 Indian schools, overseeing schools run by Indian tribes, and subsidizing public schools attended by Indians.

Ivan Sidney, chairman of the Hopi Indian tribal council, holds a press conference in 1976. Under the federal government's current Indian policy, known as self-determination, the BIA encourages tribal governments to assume greater responsibility for their own affairs.

of Indian policy was coexistence with Indians, the BIA oversaw trade with Indian tribes, negotiated peace treaties, purchased Indian land, and distributed annual federal payments to Indians. After the government changed its emphasis during the 1830s to relocating eastern tribes to areas west of the Mississippi, the BIA helped convince several tribes to give up their ancestral homelands. The 1850s and 1860s saw tremendous growth for the BIA as the government moved scores of tribes to reservations, where the BIA took charge of the Indians' activities. During the rest of the 19th century, the BIA gradually expanded the services that it provided for reservation Indians.

Starting in 1887, under the General Allotment Act, the government broke up many reservations into individual farms as a way of inducing Indians to assimilate, or blend, into the larger society. During this so-called allotment period, which lasted until 1934, the BIA was in charge of dividing Indian land into small plots, moving Indians onto the new land, and selling surplus

18

territory. After Congress passed the Indian Reorganization Act in 1934, ending the allotment period and providing for Indians to govern themselves, the BIA helped tribes set up their own governments and businesses.

Under the current policy, which is called self-determination and which was developed under presidents Lyndon B. Johnson and Richard M. Nixon, the BIA is, in theory, committed to correcting the abuses of the past. Nevertheless, it continues to be plagued by charges of corruption, mismanagement, and insensitivity to Indian concerns.

Meanwhile, the troubles of the Indians persist. Indians fare worse than all other ethnic groups in the country in almost every economic and health category. According to the *Washington Post*, more than 14 percent of Indians who live on reservations make less than $2,500 (the figure is 5 percent for the whole U.S. population), and only 6 percent earn $30,000 or more (compared with 20 percent for the United States as whole). Reservation Indians have the highest rates of teenage suicide, alcoholism, and adult diabetes of any group in the country. Clearly, as the BIA heads into the 1990s, its task remains a difficult one.

Dutch settlers conclude a peace treaty with American Indians during the 1600s. When they first encountered Indians in the New World, Europeans sought friendship and cooperation, realizing that the aboriginal people, if united, could wipe out their small settlements.

TWO

The Origins of
Indian Policy

When European settlers arrived in North America during the 17th century, between 1 and 2 million Indians lived there. The native Americans were a diverse group of peoples, divided into hundreds of tribes that were distinguished by marked differences in language, religion, and culture. Some tribes maintained a nomadic way of life, roaming the continent's wide terrain, subsisting on berries, wild grass seeds, nuts, fish, and game. Others inhabited pueblos (dwellings made from adobe, a sun-dried building material of earth and straw) and grew corn and other vegetables. On the whole, North American Indians were not as advanced as South and Central American tribes, such as the Maya who surpassed the Greeks and Romans in their grasp of science and mathematics. Nevertheless, the political, social, and religious institutions of many North American Indians were quite sophisticated. For instance, the Iroquois League, a federation of several northeastern bands, developed procedures for resolving governmental disputes that foreshadowed methods currently used by the U.S. Congress in hammering out compromise versions of legislation. In general, Indian tribes were held together by kinship ties, unlike most European communities, which were united by mutual connections to geographical areas.

White settlers massacre Indian women and children at a settlement on the frontier. Over the course of the 17th century, violent incidents became increasingly common on the frontier as relations between Indians and settlers were strained by disagreements over trade and land sales.

The presence of Indians made little difference to European settlers as they landed in the New World. From the beginning, the Europeans' plan was to colonize and develop for their own purposes what they saw as a vast, empty land. Indians, when their existence was even acknowledged, were perceived as a savage people, a people whose rustic life-style and ignorance of Christianity made them seem inferior to Europeans and less worthy of claiming the continent's vast resources.

In spite of this attitude, the first encounters between Europeans and Indians were amicable. Indians assisted the newcomers in establishing settlements and taught them techniques for cultivating native foods. In turn, Europeans provided Indians with products they had never seen before—pots, pans, blankets, rum, rifles, gunpowder, and commercially manufactured beads and feathers. A healthy system of trade developed, with the settlers supplying manufactured goods to the Indians in exchange for animal furs, which commanded a high price back in Europe.

Gradually, however, as the settlers grew in number, trouble developed. Much of it was rooted in conflicting conceptions of land ownership. The settlers were accustomed to dividing all available land into separate parcels that were apportioned among private owners. By contrast, Indians saw their land as a communal resource and divided it among individuals only on a temporary basis for the purposes of hunting or farming. In fact, many tribes saw their control of land not as true ownership but as a loan from the gods. If a tribe vacated part of its land, other tribes were usually welcome to use it. Consequently, the boundaries of tribal land holdings tended not to be clearly defined. As European settlers began staking claims to pieces of North America, many felt an obligation to buy the land from the native inhabitants. But more often than not, because of contrasting conceptions of land ownership, the parties in land purchases had difficulty understanding each other.

Conflict over land sales produced bitterness on both sides. Colonists stirred up further ill will, on many occasions, by simply taking over Indian land without compensation. Trade with the Indians was marred by similarly unscrupulous behavior. To make matters worse, thousands of Indians were killed off by the colonists' diseases—smallpox, measles, tuberculosis, chicken pox, and scarlet fever. Even when the colonists intended to help the Indians—for instance, by introducing among them farmers, teachers, blacksmiths, and carpenters to pass on European ways—they often caused resentment.

As a climate of hostility developed on the frontier, each side began launching attacks against the other's settlements. One of the first such attacks occurred in 1637, when inhabitants of the Connecticut colony massacred more than 600 Pequot Indians in retaliation for the Indians' alleged murder of a white trader. In 1657, an Indian named Metacom (also known as King Philip) formed an alliance of several northeastern tribes to resist the colonists' encroachment. During the ensuing 20 years, the group attacked more than 50 colonial settlements, in a campaign known as King Philip's War. Toward the end of the 17th century, similar fighting broke out between colonists and Indians in Virginia and New York.

British Indian Policy

Amid this turmoil, the British government paid little attention to Indian affairs. Until the middle of the 18th century, each colony was on its own in dealing with the Indians. Each negotiated its own peace treaties and made its own land purchases. This arrangement resulted in wild inconsistencies in policy. Some of

23

the colonies were openly hostile to the Indians; others were friendlier but tried to promote European ways, sending teachers and missionaries to live among the Indians.

During the mid-1750s, however, as conflicts between France and England over territories in North America threatened to escalate into war, British leaders took a sudden interest in improving relations with the Indians. They understood that if such a war developed, the Indians, with their relatively large population and superior fighting abilities, would be useful allies. In an attempt to enlist the Indians' support, the British government increased its contacts with tribal leaders. In June 1754, British officials arranged for representatives of seven colonies to meet with the Iroquois tribe in Albany, New York. Colonial leaders greeted Indians with ceremonial declarations of esteem and showered them with gifts—scarlet coats, silver buttons, axes, scissors, and guns. But although the Indians were flattered by the gifts, they made it clear that they preferred France's Indian policy, which for several years had stressed active involvement—the construction of forts for Indian protection, the maintenance of trading posts in Indian country, and the assignment of teams of missionaries to live among the Indians.

After the Indians left the Albany Congress, as it became known, colonial delegates discussed the idea of forming an intercolonial union to conduct Indian relations. Ultimately, they adopted a plan proposed by Pennsylvania delegate Benjamin Franklin. Known as the Albany Plan of Union, it called for establishment of a central colonial government that would have authority not only over Indian affairs but also over defense and western expansion. The plan was later rejected by colonial assemblies, which were reluctant to forfeit any of their power to a central government. Nevertheless, the idea that Indian affairs be centrally administered would be suggested again.

After the Albany Congress, the British, convinced by their experience with the Iroquois that drastic measures were needed, assumed sole control over Indian affairs and for the first time established a coherent Indian policy. The policy had three goals: to clarify the boundaries of Indian land holdings by negotiating treaties; to exert government influence in the fur trade in order to prevent unscrupulous traders from cheating Indians; and to recruit Indian allies for the French and Indian War (Seven Years' War).

At the end of the war, in 1763, England's king George III issued a proclamation that expressed his nation's commitment to protecting Indian property rights. It read, "The several nations or tribes of nations, with whom we are connected, should not be molested or disturbed in the possession of such parts of our dominions and territories, as, not having been ceded to, or purchased by us, are reserved to them, or any of them, as hunting grounds." The proclamation also provided for the appointment of two British superintendents—one for the northern colonies and one for the southern colonies—to oversee "all relations between the English colonists and the Indians." The two superintendents played primarily a diplomatic role, concluding a series of treaties with the Indians.

Colonial Indian Policy

In April 1775, the first shots in the revolutionary war were fired. The Continental Congress sought to organize colonial defenses and, in one of its first actions, established a Committee on Indian Affairs to examine strategies for dealing with the Indians. After a month, the committee concluded that three Indian departments—northern, middle, and southern—should be set up to take

Indian riflemen serving in the French army overrun a British stronghold during the French and Indian War (1754–63). The British government established its first coherent Indian policy at the beginning of this war in an attempt to secure Indian military support.

the place of the British superintendencies. Congress quickly approved the plan, assigning the Northern Department to handle relations with the Iroquois, Delaware, Wyandot, and Ottawa tribes, the Middle Department to deal with the Chickasaw and Shawnee, and the Southern Department to deal with the Cherokee, Creek, Choctaw, and Seminole. Each department was headed by a group of commissioners. During the war, several illustrious colonial leaders served as commissioners, including Benjamin Franklin and Patrick Henry. Congress was given final authority in Indian affairs.

The primary goal of colonial Indian policy was to convince Indian tribes either to support the American Revolution or to remain neutral in the conflict.

During the revolutionary war, Benjamin Franklin served as commissioner of one of the regional departments set up by the Continental Congress to handle relations with the Indians.

26

Commissioners were instructed to seek out Indian leaders and to negotiate treaties of friendship and military alliance. The colonial government concluded its first treaty with the Delaware Indians on September 17, 1778. Among other provisions, the treaty raised for the first time the possibility that American leaders would eventually create a separate state for Indians.

In general, however, the colonies enjoyed much less success than the British in recruiting Indians as military allies. Several tribes, including the Iroquois, made significant contributions to the British war effort. In 1779, colonial General John Sullivan demonstrated American frustration with the lack of Indian support, leading 4,000 troops in attacking Iroquois settlements, razing hundreds of brick houses, demolishing lush gardens of corn, beans, and melon, and, in the words of historian William Hagar, "blighting one of the most advanced Indian societies in North America."

After the war ended in 1783, the Indian departments continued to operate. Their role had been significantly reduced, however, by the Articles of Confederation, passed by Congress in 1777 and ratified by the states in 1781. Under Article 9, the federal government had the power to manage Indian affairs and to regulate Indian trade "provided that the legislative rights of any state within its own limits be not infringed or violated." In effect, this meant that the federal government no longer had authority in Indian affairs except in territories not yet incorporated as states. As a result, commissioners found it virtually impossible to prevent settlers, trappers, and land speculators from violating federal laws passed during the early 1780s to protect Indian property rights.

The Indian Department

In 1786 Congress revamped the organization that did business with Indians. Under a bill called the Ordinance of 1786, the Middle Department was eliminated and its territory was divided between the two remaining departments. The Southern District was defined to include all the Indian nations south of the Ohio River. The Northern District extended over the Indian nations west of the Hudson River. Responsibility for running each district was given to a single official, a superintendent of Indian affairs. Appointed by Congress, each superintendent was to serve a two-year term and was required to live in his own district. The two superintendents, together with their field staffs, were given status as a new agency called the Indian Department. Unlike all of today's government departments, it did not have an office in the nation's capital. Nevertheless, it provided the framework for what would eventually become

In 1786, Arthur St. Clair became the first superintendent of the Northern District, one of two regional divisions within the Indian Department.

the Bureau of Indian Affairs. The department was put under the supervision of the secretary of war, who was required to keep in close contact with the two superintendents and to prepare regular reports on their activities.

The first person to be appointed superintendent of Indian affairs for the Southern District was James White, who had served as a captain of the militia during the American Revolution. Arthur St. Clair, who was already serving as governor of the Western Territory, took over responsibility for the Northern District. For the most part, St. Clair and White performed specific tasks outlined in detail by directives from Congress. The majority of these tasks involved overseeing trade between settlers and Indians on the frontier and resolving disputes that frequently developed between the two groups. Gradually, the superintendents became responsible for a new federal policy—the acquisition of Indian land. During colonial times, most land acquired from the Indians had been purchased or taken by individual settlers. But, as St. Clair and White took office, an increasing number of Indians were being forced off their land without compensation, frequently resulting in military conflicts that required the intercession of the U.S. Army. Disturbed by this development— out of concern for Indian rights and distress at rising military costs—Congress ordered the superintendents to monitor land transactions closely. On a number of occasions, when it became apparent that white settlers meant to appropriate Indian territory by force, the superintendents were instructed to intercede and to negotiate with the Indians for title to the land. Money, goods, or services were provided in exchange. The Indian Department was also instructed to compensate tribes that had previously been cheated in land deals.

In the Northwest Ordinance, passed in 1787, Congress transformed its concern for the property rights of Indians into a formal commitment. In that law, Congress declared: "The utmost good faith shall always be observed toward Indians; their lands and property shall never be taken from them without their consent; and in their property, rights, and liberty, they shall never be invaded or disturbed, unless in just and lawful wars authorized by Congress." It was the first time that the federal government had promised to treat Indians in a fair and humane manner. Later reaffirmed by the Constitution, the Northwest Ordinance remains in effect today. It has inspired numerous aid and education programs that have benefited the Indians, though it has been violated repeatedly. In the first years after its passage, the ordinance was largely ignored by whites on the frontier.

Expansion of Federal Power

By the time the Constitutional Convention was convened in the summer of 1787, the founding fathers were determined to expand the federal government's authority in the area of Indian affairs. Without federal control, convention delegates felt, exploitation of Indian property rights would continue and might lead to a major military conflict. The young nation remained small enough that its very existence would have been threatened by a full-scale war with the Indians (provided the Indians could have overcome traditional rivalries to form a united army). The Constitution was completed in September 1787, ratified by most states in 1788, and put into effect in 1789. In Article I, Section 8, the Constitution granted Congress power to regulate commerce with Indian tribes. Portions of the document dealing with foreign affairs further extended federal power over Indian policy without referring specifically to Indians. The president was authorized to receive envoys from and make treaties with foreign nations, subject to the Senate's approval. These powers applied to interactions with Indians because at the time Indian tribes were considered foreign nations.

After the Constitution took effect in 1789, the new nation's leaders decided that the secretary of war should continue to oversee the implementation of Indian policy. On August 7, 1789, Congress passed an act creating the War Department and stipulating that the secretary of war would perform "such duties as shall from time to time be enjoined on, or entrusted to him by the president of the United States, agreeably to the Constitution, relative to Indian affairs." To carry out Indian policy in the field, the apparatus set up by the Ordinance of 1786 was kept intact.

The first president of the United States, George Washington, and his secretary of war, Henry Knox, were determined to establish friendly relations with Indian tribes. Doing so was considered vital to national security for several reasons. First, periodic skirmishes with Indians on the frontier were draining military resources and preventing the nation from securing its borders. Second, the possibility of an all-out war with Indians had increased, as several tribes had taken up arms against the colonies, determined to drive settlers back to the Atlantic Ocean. Furthermore, the Indians represented a key variable in the balance of power among European nations with holdings on the North American continent. In 1789, the military weakness of the United States and the nation's bounteous natural resources made it a likely target for attack by England or Spain. In any controversy between the United States and a European aggressor, the support of the Indians would be crucial.

Trade and Intercourse Acts

The best way to strengthen ties with Indian tribes, Knox and Washington decided, was to improve trade relations. Trade relations had recently become strained, however, by white merchants' widespread use of unfair practices. To correct these abuses and to gain the trust and esteem of Indians, the Washington administration sought to exert greater federal control over commerce with the Indians. Toward this end, it steered through Congress a series of bills known to history as the Trade and Intercourse Acts.

The first Trade and Intercourse Act, passed on July 2, 1790, stipulated that anyone wishing to engage in trade with Indians had to obtain a license from the federal government. To acquire a license, a trader had to file an application with one of the superintendents of Indian affairs and post a $1,000 bond. Superintendents had authority to revoke a trader's license if he failed to comply with trade regulations established by the president. The act also prohibited individuals from purchasing land from Indians unless they did so under a treaty negotiated by the government. Finally, the act established procedures for the arrest and trial of traders accused of committing crimes against Indians in areas outside the 13 existing states.

The second Trade and Intercourse Act, passed in 1793, prohibited white settlements on Indian land. It also set up rules to govern the horse trade and empowered the superintendents to impose penalties on horse thieves. The third Trade and Intercourse Act, enacted in 1796, prohibited whites from driving livestock on Indian land and required those traveling through Indian territory to carry passports.

Each of these acts was intended to remain in effect for only two years. But on March 30, 1802, Congress passed a permanent Trade and Intercourse Act that included most of the provisions of the earlier acts. This law served as the foundation for federal Indian policy until 1830. Its only new provision authorized the president to regulate and, if necessary, prohibit the sale of liquor to Indians. With this provision, Congress meant not to punish Indians but to protect them from being swindled. Indians had a low tolerance for alcohol, having never encountered the substance prior to the arrival of the Europeans. Nevertheless, they enjoyed liquor and traded for it regularly. Unscrupulous white businessmen frequently took advantage of Indians' difficult relationship with alcohol, plying them with whiskey or rum during trade negotiations and then, once the Indians were too drunk to think clearly, convincing them to accept unfair terms. On not a few occasions, Indians awoke from drunken stupors to find they had traded away all their possessions in exchange for a few bottles of "firewater."

Henry Knox, secretary of war from 1785 to 1794, was given control of the Indian Department by the Ordinance of 1786. With the approval of Congress, the final authority on Indian affairs under the Constitution, Knox helped establish coexistence as the goal of federal Indian policy.

The Indian Department was put in charge of enforcing the Trade and Intercourse Acts, and as a result expanded considerably during the 1790s. Much of this growth took place among the department's staff of agents and subagents, officials who lived with Indian tribes and set policy in motion on the local level. Reporting either to the War Department or to superintendents, agents carried out such tasks as removing trespassers from Indian land, checking traders for licenses, and monitoring liquor sales. New agent positions were created in a number of ways—by order of a superintendent, by legislative act, or in many cases, by the terms of a treaty with Indians. By order of Secretary Knox, many of those hired as agents by the Indian Department were missionaries, who were thought to have greater success than government officials in gaining the trust of Indians.

Trading Houses

As the 1790s proceeded, it became clear that federal efforts to reform commerce with the Indians were achieving only limited success. Many traders continued to operate without licenses and persisted in cheating Indians; licensed traders were forced to follow their lead in order to compete in the marketplace. Eventually, President Washington decided that the government itself should trade with the Indians. He conceived the notion of the trading house—a frontier outpost at which government personnel would provide Indians with supplies in a strictly regulated manner. Such trading houses, he argued, would help the government gain the trust of the Indians and at the same time enable it to exert greater control over commerce.

On April 18, 1796, Congress granted Washington's wish, authorizing the president to establish such outposts wherever he desired and appropriating $150,000 for that purpose. Between 1796 and 1801, the government set up seven trading houses. Operating on a not-for-profit basis, the trading houses offered, in return for furs, such goods as pots, pans, rifles, powder, and blankets. By offering higher prices than most private traders did, the trading houses acquired a sizable portion of the markets in their areas. But the trading house system was not without its problems. For one thing, locations were chosen to suit the government and were often inconvenient for Indian clients. In addition, some tribes were scared away from trading houses by the government's custom of stationing federal troops nearby—although usually this was done to protect against invasion by European armies.

With the creation of the trading house system, it became impossible for just two superintendents to supervise all of the Indian Department's activities.

Consequently, in the late 1790s the Northern and Southern districts were dissolved, the superintendents' positions were eliminated, and authority formerly wielded by the superintendents was transferred to territorial governors—officials who administered regions controlled by the United States but not yet incorporated as states. This system remained in place throughout the period of expansion to the West during the 1800s. Each time a new territorial government was set up, its governor was required to double as head of Indian affairs for his district.

Negotiating Treaties

In the early 1800s, the Indian Department began to play a larger role in negotiating treaties. A decade earlier, on August 20, 1789, Congress had transferred primary authority for negotiating treaties from the superintendents

Indians exchange furs for commercially manufactured products at a frontier store. During the 1790s, American leaders attempted to strengthen ties with the Indians by improving trade relations.

33

of Indian affairs (with whom it had resided under the Ordinance of 1786) to peace commissioners, members of temporary bargaining teams appointed by the president prior to each peace conference. Superintendents had assisted the commissioners, who worked independently of the Indian Department, only in making sure tribal representatives were assembled for talks at appointed times and places. But, in the early 1800s, several territorial governors, working without congressional sanction, established themselves as equal partners to the peace commissioners in the negotiating process. Between 1800 and 1812, the governor of the Indiana Territory, William Henry Harrison (who in 1841 would become the ninth president of the United States), helped conclude 15 treaties. These pacts gave the nation possession of territory that would eventually compose much of Indiana and Illinois and parts of Ohio, Michigan, and Wisconsin.

Many different types of Indian treaties were made during this period. Some were merely declarations of peace between the United States and particular tribes; these usually included clauses calling for the prosecution of "bad men," members of either side who violated the peace. Other treaties recognized tribes' claims to certain pieces of land and granted tribes permanent title to the tracts. (In later years, many reservations were created by this kind of treaty.) Most treaties, however, involved the federal government's purchase of Indian land. The treaties' terms of sale varied widely, but usually they involved the payment of annuities—payments made annually for long periods of time. The treaty that the Indian Department concluded with several tribes on September 29, 1817, provided examples of various types of annuities. According to this treaty, the Wyandot were to receive yearly payments of $4,000 for as long as the federal government existed; the Seneca, $500 a year forever; the Shawnee, $2,000 a year forever; the Potawatomi, $1,300 a year for 15 years; the Ottowa, $1,000 a year for 15 years; and the Chippewa, $1,000 a year for 15 years.

Emergence of New Indian Policies

During its first three decades, the Indian Department concentrated most of its efforts on diplomacy, trade relations, and land purchase. The primary goal of federal Indian policy during this period was peaceful coexistence with the American natives. But at the same time, two completely opposite approaches to Indian policy gradually gained support among federal officials and occasionally

Federal officials sign a treaty with the Sioux Indians. During the early 1800s, the Indian Department began to play a role in negotiating treaties with the Indians, arranging for declarations of peace, land sales, and acknowledgments of Indian land rights.

received expression in Indian Department activities. These approaches called for (1) the removal of Indians to territory in the west and (2) the assimilation (the complete absorption of one group into another group's cultural tradition) of Indians into white society.

President Thomas Jefferson first put forth the idea of removal in 1803 after purchasing from France a huge tract of land on the west side of the Mississippi. Called Louisiana, the territory doubled the size of the United States. In Jefferson's view, the Louisiana Purchase put the country in control of sufficient land and resources to fill the needs both of whites and Indians. The best way to divide up the land, he suggested, would be to relocate Indians to the area west of the Mississippi and have non-Indians remain east of the river. Separating the two groups, Jefferson maintained, would reduce conflict and enable the country to spend less money and energy on Indian affairs. In an 1804 act incorporating the new land as the Louisiana Territory, Congress included, at Jefferson's insistence, a clause authorizing the president to seek treaties in which Indians ceded their land in exchange for holdings west of the Mississippi. During Jefferson's presidency only one tribe was "removed" in this manner— 2,000 members of the Cherokee tribe were relocated from Tennessee to

Arkansas. But between 1815 and 1820, several more tribes succumbed to government pressure. Other tribes moved west of their own accord—primarily to seek larger quantities of game. With the development of the fur trade, Indians had begun hunting far more intensively than before the arrival of the white man—when they hunted only for food—and they had severely depleted game reserves in many eastern areas. By 1820, several tribes, including the Narragansett, Mohican, Pequot, and Delaware had been drastically reduced in population in eastern coastal areas, having either been victimized by the government's fledgling removal program or wiped out by disease.

Meanwhile, in dealing with other tribes—such as the Cherokee and the Delaware—the government pursued what was known as "civilization" policy. Under this policy, the BIA attempted to teach Indians European ways in an effort to assimilate them into the dominant society. Agents negotiated treaties that called for leatherworkers, masons, blacksmiths, and other specialists to live among the Indians to teach them European crafts. A major element of the policy was the establishment of schools where Indian youth received instruction in the standard European curriculum. In 1819, Congress established an annual appropriation of $10,000 for "civilization." The appropriation, which remained in effect until 1873, was used primarily to pay various missionary organizations hired by the government to construct and operate schools for Indian children. The Indian Department oversaw the disbursement of the funds.

The federal government's pursuit of three radically different approaches to Indian affairs reflected several factors—disagreement among policymakers, the diversity of the Indian population, and the difficulty of making Indian policy. The simultaneous operation of several policies would remain a characteristic of federal Indian policy throughout the 1800s.

Growing Pains

In charge of paying annuities, administering "civilization" programs, negotiating treaties, running trading houses, and enforcing the Trade and Intercourse Acts, the Indian Department grew significantly during its first three decades. Between 1791 and 1822, its budget rose from $39,424 to $123,638. The latter figure was at that time a significant portion of the overall federal budget. By 1822, the department was responsible for distributing $468,251 in annuities.

Meanwhile, Congress doubled its allocation for trading houses from $150,000 to $300,000. As the trading house system expanded, the Indian Department was often forced to solicit the aid of other government divisions. The job of hauling supplies from eastern industrial centers to trading houses on the frontier was often assigned to the U.S. Army. The Purveyor of Public Supplies helped purchase the goods sold by trading houses and the Comptroller of the Treasury helped keep trading house books in order. The division of responsibility for Indian trade among three agencies often produced confusion and delays. In 1806, Congress attempted to make the regulation of Indian trade more efficient by setting up a separate division of the Indian Department called the Trade Department and establishing the position of superintendent of Indian trade. With a staff of several clerks and messengers, the trade superintendent was given an office in the War Department building in Washington, D.C.—the first time the Indian Department had a central office. Thomas L. McKenney, an energetic official who became superintendent of Indian trade in 1816, extended the powers of his position, establishing himself as de facto (that is, not recognized by law) coordinator of Indian affairs.

Expansion created problems for the department in the area of bookkeeping. According to the terms of a 1796 act of Congress, the War Department's accountant was assigned to disburse funds to buy goods sold at trading houses and pay annuities, either in cash or in the form of goods. But as the number of Indian treaties increased, the accountant became overwhelmed with work. According to an 1816 report on the department's finances, not a single account had been completely settled since 1796. War Department officials also had difficulty keeping up with administrative tasks in other areas of Indian affairs.

On May 6, 1822, Congress lightened the War Department's administrative workload for Indian affairs by disbanding the trading house system, despite several government studies that found trading houses to be efficiently run and popular with the Indians. In making the decision, federal legislators were influenced by the lobbying efforts of private traders, who had lost much of their business to the trading houses, and by fur companies, which were dismayed by the rise in fur prices resulting from the government's involvement in Indian trade. In the same bill, Congress disbanded the Indian Trade Department and terminated the contract of trade superintendent McKenney.

Even after the trading houses were closed, the War Department continued to be swamped with Indian affairs work. Meanwhile, it became clear that the Treasury Department, the State Department, and other government bureaus were similarly overburdened. Eventually, the heads of all the departments agreed to urge Congress to establish a new cabinet-level department, the Home Department, to perform tasks existing departments were unable to handle, including management of the Indian Department, the Post Office, and the Patent Office.

Creation of the BIA

By 1824, however, the secretary of war, John C. Calhoun, became convinced that the proposal would never become a reality. On March 11, he took matters into his own hands, reorganizing the Indian Department as an independent branch of the War Department and renaming it the Bureau of Indian Affairs. Given its own director, Thomas L. McKenney, and several new clerks—in addition to the staff it inherited from the Indian Department—the new bureau took over all Indian affairs tasks formerly performed by the secretary of war and his aides.

Calhoun's establishment of a federal bureau on his own initiative was an unorthodox course of action. At the time, most organizations that executed laws passed by Congress—departments, bureaus, independent offices, commissions, authorities, and boards—were established by acts of Congress. Lack of congressional involvement in the bureau's creation meant that no federal monies were specifically appropriated for the agency's use. Therefore, to fund the bureau's new activities and to pay its new employees, Calhoun had to transfer to the BIA the salaries of War Department jobs that had been vacated.

At first there were no objections to Calhoun's new bureau. Gradually, however, officials realized that for Indian affairs to be conducted efficiently,

In 1824, Secretary of War John C. Calhoun revamped the Indian Department. He made it a separate division of the War Department, transferred to it all of the War Department's responsibilities for Indian policy, and renamed it the Bureau of Indian Affairs.

McKenney's appointment needed to be placed on a firmer legal footing. The 1789 act creating the War Department had delegated the president's authority for Indian affairs to the secretary of war, but the legislation had not authorized the secretary in turn to delegate that authority to another official. Without any legal authority, McKenney could attend to the details of Indian affairs but could not act for the secretary. Thus, every piece of correspondence, every decision, every disbursement, and every claim settlement had to come before the secretary of war for final approval. Of course, this situation created a serious administrative bottleneck and severely limited McKenney's powers. In 1832, Congress gave the head of the BIA a new title, commissioner of Indian affairs, and power to make final decisions. By this time, McKenney had been dismissed by President Andrew Jackson and replaced by Elbert Herring.

Having become familiar with the BIA's problems, Congress soon launched a thorough investigation of the agency's activities. From 1832 to 1834, members of the House Committee on Indian Affairs conducted the probe. In the process, they discovered that the bureau's lack of congressional sanction caused serious administrative and budgetary difficulties. They also found that there was no legal basis for the system of agents and subagents, and that the provisions of the Trade and Intercourse Acts that provided for the appointment of agents were not intended to make the agencies permanent institutions. In response to these findings, Congress passed a bill on June 30, 1834, that recognized the independent status of the BIA. The measure also established procedures for the hiring of agents. It did not, however, change the bureau's duties or the structure of its national office.

Escorted by federal troops, Cherokee Indians are forced to walk 800 miles from their ancestral lands in Georgia to a new home in Arkansas in 1838. The painful exodus, known to history as the "Trail of Tears," was one of many tragedies that resulted from the government's decision to relocate all eastern tribes to areas west of the Mississippi River.

THREE

"The Trail of Tears"

Four years before Congress made the BIA an official agency, the federal government had shifted the emphasis of its Indian policy from coexistence to removal. The shift was prompted by several factors: the diminishing supply of land available east of the Mississippi for new settlers; the increasing number of violent incidents between Indians and non-Indians on the frontier; the popularity of the concept of manifest destiny (the notion that the United States was destined, even entitled, to expand its western borders to the Pacific Ocean); and pressure from state governments to eliminate Indians from their territories. Events in the state of Georgia provided the final impetus for the policy change.

Removal

In 1802, the federal government had made a pact with Georgia to remove all Indians from the state at some future date in return for Georgia's cession of its western territories to the United States. In the 1820s, when the government still had not fulfilled its part of the deal, Georgia's leaders grew impatient. Seeking more land for cotton plantations, they confiscated, on their own, land belonging to the Creek and Cherokee Indians. To the federal government's chagrin, the state also passed laws authorizing officials to harass the eastern Cherokee, and it nullified the Cherokee nation's constitution, a document modeled after the U.S. Constitution. The motivation for the latter action was the fear that the more civilized the Indians became, the harder it would be to uproot them from their homelands. The Supreme Court, under Chief Justice John Marshall, would several years later, in *Worcester v. Georgia* (1832), declare Georgia's campaign against Indians unlawful, ruling that the federal government had sole jurisdiction in the area of Indian affairs.

In the meantime, however, Andrew Jackson, a strong supporter of removal, took office as president in 1829. Jackson was determined to resolve the burgeoning dispute between the federal government and Georgia, which was threatening to secede if a federal removal program were not begun immediately. In his first message to Congress, Jackson, who in 1808 had helped negotiate the first relocation treaty with the Cherokees, endorsed legislation

Under Chief Justice John Marshall, the Supreme Court handed down two key rulings regarding Indian policy. It decided in 1831 that Indians should be considered wards of the government rather than separate nations, and, in 1832, that the federal government, not the states, had authority over Indian affairs.

42

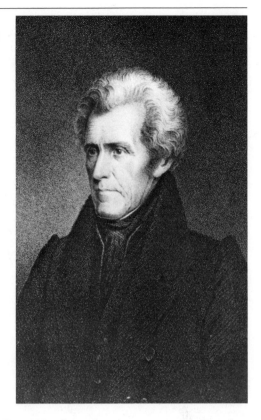

In 1830, President Andrew Jackson convinced Congress to pass the Indian Removal Bill, the cornerstone of removal policy. Within 15 years, the majority of eastern tribes had been forced west of the Mississippi.

calling for voluntary removal. In 1830, Congress went even further than Jackson had requested, passing the Indian Removal Act, which called for all eastern Indians to give up their land in exchange for holdings in unsettled territory west of the Mississippi. Under the bill, Indians were told that if they refused to evacuate, they would no longer be protected by the federal government against the states. Supporters of the bill insisted that it would benefit Indians by putting distance between them and non-Indian settlers bent on their annihilation. Provisions in the bill authorized the president to protect the Indians in their new tribal areas, to pay them for improvements they had made on their old land, and to subsidize their move and their first year's expenses in the west.

Jackson argued that the Indian Removal Act placed Indians in a situation where they would "share in the blessings of civilization and be saved from the degradation and destruction to which they were rapidly hastening while they remained in the states." But many Americans opposed this view, arguing that

43

Black Hawk (left), a Sauk and Fox warrior, and Osceola (right), a Seminole chief, both led valiant but ultimately unsuccessful uprisings against removal.

separating Indians from their homelands would cause severe economic and psychological hardship. In fact, the removal policy resulted in deep divisions in American society—among members of Congress, in the press, and among Indians themselves.

As it turned out, removal had a devastating effect on the Indians. The first treaty negotiated and ratified under the Indian Removal Bill was the Treaty of Dancing Rabbit Creek, signed by the Choctaw tribe on September 27, 1830. Nearly destroyed by disease and war, the Choctaws reluctantly accepted the pact, knowing that otherwise they would face almost certain defeat at the hands of Georgian settlers. Their chief, David Folsom, remarked afterward, "We are exceedingly tired. Our doom is sealed. There is no other course for us but to turn our focus to our new houses toward the setting sun."

The removal of the Cherokees was particularly brutal. In 1838, more than 17,000 Cherokees were rounded up by Georgia militiamen. The helpless Indians were forced to travel, by steamboat, crowded boxcar, and by foot, to Arkansas, 800 miles from their home. During the march, known to history as the "Trail of Tears," 4,000 Cherokees died of disease, starvation, and exposure.

Many tribes in the southern and northern states moved voluntarily— because of persuasion, bribery, and threats. But a few tribes put up fierce resistance. In 1832, a portion of the Sauk and Fox tribe, under the leadership of a young warrior named Black Hawk, refused to comply with a relocation agreement negotiated by their chief Keokuk. Although the majority of the Sauk and Fox trekked from their home in Wisconsin to new territory in Iowa, Black Hawk led his band in armed revolt against federal troops assigned to oversee removal. After conducting several bloody raids against white settlements and eluding capture for several months, the rebels were finally overcome by the U.S. Army at the Battle of Bad Axe River on August 3, 1832.

The Seminole Indians of Florida staged a similar uprising. Led by a chief named Osceola, the Seminoles ambushed a company of federal troops on December 28, 1835, killing all 107 of the company's members. Afterward, Osceola sent a letter to army leaders, saying "You have guns, and so have we—you have powder and lead, and so have we—you have men and so have we—your men will fight, so will ours, till the last drop of the Seminole's blood has moistened the dust of his hunting grounds." Not until 1842 were the Seminoles finally defeated and dislodged from their territory. Even then several hundred Seminoles escaped the army and retreated into the Everglades.

Portions of a few other Indian tribes, including part of the eastern Cherokee, managed to avoid removal. But by the mid-1840s, a large number of tribes that once inhabited the eastern United States had been forced to move to areas west of the Mississippi River.

What role did the BIA play in removal policy? In 1830, lobbying by BIA head Thomas McKenney helped convince Congress to adopt the Indian Removal Act. In 1834, the BIA began playing a part in carrying out the policy after Congress gave the bureau permanent status. Under orders from President Jackson, the BIA assumed responsibility for negotiating removal treaties. The BIA's first commissioner of Indian affairs, Elbert Herring, pursued this mission with exceptional vigor. "In the consummation of this grand and sacred object [removal] rests the sole chance of averting Indian annihilation," he declared. Ultimately, however, the BIA's diplomatic activities proved far less effective in convincing Indians to abandon their homelands than the U.S. Army's threats and use of force. As a consequence, the BIA held a subordinate position to the army during the removal period.

Between 1830 and 1850, nearly 100,000 Indians were removed from the eastern United States. They were resettled on generous allotments of land west of the Mississippi. Their new lands constituted the first reservations, but they differed from later reservations in their vast size and loosely defined boundaries. Moreover, much of the territory provided for relocation was already inhabited by other Indian tribes. Competition among indigenous and newly settled Indians for land and game resulted in several intertribal wars.

In 1849, the BIA was transferred from the Department of War to the Department of the Interior. To remain in close contact with Indians, the BIA relocated most of its agencies to areas west of the Mississippi during the removal period.

Westward Expansion

The goal of the removal policy was to separate Indians from whites and thereby minimize conflict between the two groups. One of the assumptions on which the policy was based was that whites would be satisfied with their share of land and resources and remain confined to their designated area. But in the 1840s, the frontier advanced rapidly beyond the Mississippi, and the policy collapsed. Many settlers were drawn westward by the nation's acquisition of new territories. In 1848, the Treaty of Guadalupe Hidalgo with Mexico extended the dominion of the United States to the Pacific Ocean. The two large states of Texas and California joined the union in 1845 and 1850 respectively. And in 1853, in the Gadsden Purchase, Mexico ceded to the United States a strip of territory that included the southern parts of present-day New Mexico and Arizona. New territories offered the prospect of cheap farmland and abundant natural resources, attracting homesteaders, entrepreneurs, and adventurers. The discovery of gold in California in 1849 and in Colorado during the 1850s further stimulated westward expansion, as did the rapid growth of the nation's network of railroads.

On their way to various parts of the continent, settlers routinely trespassed upon and exploited Indian territory. Many settled in the Midwest on lands previously allotted to the Indians by the federal government. In the process, white hunters quickly succeeded in exterminating the buffalo, the animal around which the economies of Plains Indians had revolved for centuries. When Indians retaliated against white incursions by attacking wagon trains and settlements, white settlers responded in kind—eventually giving rise to an escalating cycle of terror and revenge.

American leaders realized that something had to be done to defuse frontier tensions. In evaluating alternative courses of action, they did not even consider the idea of cutting back the flow of westward migration, for by this time most Americans accepted the notion of manifest destiny. Instead, policymakers resolved to move all tribes onto reservations. This policy was to help settlers by removing Indians from the most desirable western regions. In theory, it was also supposed to benefit the Indians by providing them with clearly defined homelands where they would be safe from the depredations of the settlers.

In practice, reservations were considered extremely undesirable. In contrast to territories allotted to eastern tribes during the removal period, these reservations were situated on arid, unwanted land, provided minimal space, and were usually located hundreds of miles from the tribe's place of origin. They also lacked the spiritual meaning that ancestral homelands had. Some tribes voluntarily moved to reservations. Most of the peoples who had been moved from the east did not have the strength to resist the policy and had to give up their fertile lands on the western shore of the Mississippi and move to Oklahoma (which was then known as Indian Territory). In the west, many Pueblo Indians were given reservations on land where they had lived for

Miners pan for gold on a California hillside. Lured by the discovery of gold in California and by the nation's acquisition of new lands, pioneers streamed westward during the 1840s and 1850s, rendering futile the government's attempt to keep Indians and whites separated by the Mississippi River.

centuries and thus put up little opposition. But many hunting tribes, accustomed to roaming hundreds of miles, tracking game and raiding other tribes, resisted reservation policy with all their might.

Indian Wars, 1850–1870

The United States fought several wars with the Indians during the 1850s and 1860s. The most dramatic battles involved the Indians who inhabited the northern Plains—an area bounded on the west by the Rocky Mountains, on the east by the Missouri River, on the south by Texas, and on the north by Canada. Accustomed to a nomadic way of living that frequently brought them into armed conflict with each other over issues of land and resources, Plains Indians were extremely proficient cavalrymen. Because of the Plains Indians'

Indians ambush a wagon train. Many of the white settlers who migrated westward during the mid-1800s settled on Indian land, prompting Indians to conduct a series of retaliatory attacks against wagon trains and white settlements. To stem the tide of violence, the federal government resolved to move all Indian tribes onto reservations.

48

Sitting Bull, a Teton Sioux chief, falls from his horse after being shot and killed by federal troops in 1890. In its attempt to force Indians onto reservations, the United States fought several wars, the most dramatic of which involved the Sioux and other Plains Indians.

military prowess, the government was at first reluctant to try to bring these tribes onto reservations. Instead, officials concentrated on securing guarantees from the Indians that they would not disturb settlers traveling the Oregon Trail toward the west coast. In September 1851, near Fort Laramie, Wyoming, almost 10,000 Plains Indians made such a pledge, receiving in return promises of generous annuities and protection against attacks by settlers.

But in 1862, a period of violent conflict began when the Sioux Indians in Minnesota, fearing that they were being surrounded by white settlements, staged a fierce uprising. Although settlers eventually defeated the Indians and killed their leader, Little Crow, the federal government rushed volunteer troops to the area to prevent further unrest. In October 1864, Cheyenne Indians stirred these troops into action by cutting off the main transportation route from the east to Denver. Led by Colonel J. M. Chivington, government troops raided a peaceful encampment of Cheyenne—whose chiefs, Black Kettle and White Antelope, had in fact asked for an armistice—and killed more than 300 men, women, and children. The Chivington Massacre prompted a frenzy of retaliation across the Plains. Cheyenne, Arapaho, and Sioux Indians attacked wagon trains, ranches, and stagecoach stations. On several occasions, the Indians defeated army units sent to quell the uprisings, including an expedition of regular army troops assigned to the region in 1865, after the conclusion of the Civil War.

Realizing the difficulty of subduing the Indians through military means, government leaders instead decided to pursue treaty negotiations, offering the Plains Indians generous annuities and gifts in return for a promise to allow the construction of the Union Pacific Railroad across the Plains and a trail connecting mines in Montana to the Oregon Trail. Although many of the tribes accepted the deal, Red Cloud, a powerful Oglala Sioux chief, refused to accept the proposed mining trail. When the government proceeded with plans for the trail anyway, setting up several army forts along the proposed route, Red Cloud took to the warpath. For three years, the Oglala staged assaults against army forts, winning the majority of the battles, with the notable exception of the "wagon box fight"—a remarkable stand by settlers behind a corral of wagon boxes. By 1868, plans for a mining trail were abandoned and Red Cloud signed a peace treaty at Fort Laramie, Wyoming.

As the 1870s began, many Plains Indians continued to roam free. Indians in other regions had less success in resisting the reservation policy. Beginning in

A Sioux woman is flanked by General William T. Sherman (second from left) and other members of the Indian Peace Commission. Established by Congress in 1865, the commission negotiated many of the treaties under which tribes were required to live on reservations.

the late 1830s, tribes in Texas faced threats to their existence. For three decades, the Kiowa and the Comanche fought off settlers and the U.S. Army. By 1867, the tribes had been forced to move to Indian country. In California, settlers subdued most of the Indians without army assistance. Gold miners who swept into the state in droves in the 1840s repeatedly overran Indian settlements. When the Indians responded with ambushes, they were massacred by the thousands. In the 1850s, 70,000 Californian Indians died from disease and warfare. The survivors were herded onto reservations in the undesirable parts of the state. Several northwestern tribes, including the Yakima, Coeur d'Alene, Spokane, and Nisqually, were forced onto reservations in the 1850s after a series of wars with the U.S. Army and the Washington State militia.

Tribes defeated by the U.S. Army were forced to sign peace treaties under which they were required to move to reservations and to relinquish huge quantities of land. In the years between 1853 and 1856 alone, the United States acquired title to more than 174 million acres of Indian land. After the Civil War, many of the treaties were secured by the Indian Peace Commission, a seven-member panel created by Congress in 1865 to quiet tensions on the frontier. Members of the commission included BIA head Nathaniel G. Taylor and U.S. Army general William Tecumseh Sherman.

Reservations

As scores of Indian tribes moved onto reservations in the 1850s and 1860s, the BIA became responsible for overseeing their activities. On each reservation, the bureau set up an agency consisting of an office building, a school, a dormitory, barns, stables, storehouses, and housing for BIA employees. One of the BIA's primary duties on reservations was to provide economic assistance, for while in theory reservations were supposed to have enough resources for Indians to live self-sufficiently, in practice there was often too little game and land fit for farming to feed every member of a tribe.

The establishment of agencies on reservations reflected a shift in the legal status of Indians. During the nation's early years, Indian tribes were regarded as foreign nations. Then, in 1831, Chief Justice John Marshall redefined Indians' "relation to the United States as resembling that of a ward to his guardian." This view of the relationship took some time to gain wide acceptance and, in the meantime, hundreds of treaties were concluded in which Indian tribes were regarded as nations. But by 1862 Secretary of the Interior Caleb Smith had made Marshall's scheme the official policy of his department

Kaw Indian leaders meet with BIA officials in Washington, D.C., during the 1850s. By that time, the BIA had been transferred from the War Department to the Department of the Interior and had been given responsibility for managing Indian reservations.

and the BIA. From that time on, the wardship approach governed all actions of the BIA on reservations, although it did not apply to the U.S. Army in its continuing effort to secure the frontier.

As the number of reservations increased between 1850 and 1870, the BIA grew in size and significance. In taking over responsibility for reservation Indians, it assumed what would be its primary role through the next century. Between 1852 and 1872, the BIA's field staff grew by 1,000 percent. In 1852, 108 people worked for the bureau—14 in the central office and 94 in the field (as agents, subagents, interpreters, and clerks). By 1872, the field staff numbered 987 and employed 21 different types of specialists, including physicians, teachers, farmers, blacksmiths, carpenters, millers, shoemakers, gunsmiths, wagon makers, and plow makers.

In its capacity as the guardian of reservation Indians, the BIA supplied weekly food rations and clothing to many tribes. By 1872, 131,000 of the 300,000 Indians living in the United States relied entirely or partly on government aid. Many tribes continued to receive monetary annuities granted by peace treaties. Annuities ranged from $1,000 to $100,000—depending on the size of the tribe—and were divided equally among all members of each tribe rather than presented to tribal leaders in one lump sum. Payment day was an annual or semiannual event and usually was accompanied by much fanfare. Every member of the tribe congregated at the agency to receive his or her share of the annuity in *specie* (gold or silver coin money). Afterward, the cash-rich Indians shopped at stalls on the reservations set up by traders hawking such items as grains, cooking pans, pots and utensils, washtubs and washboards, coffee mills, household articles, calico blankets, clothing, salt, flour, bacon, saddles, jewelry, and bridles.

Although payment days brought temporary elation, life on the reservation was extremely difficult most of the time. In spite of government subsidies, many Indians lived in constant danger of starvation. Economic woes were

An Indian family gathers on the steps of its reservation home. Under a directive from Interior Secretary Caleb Smith, the BIA in 1862 began treating Indians as its wards, providing them with food rations, financial assistance, agricultural training, and education.

Yuma Indian men meet with a BIA agent on their reservation. In spite of BIA efforts, reservation life was very difficult. Poverty was everywhere, disease rampant, and alcoholism widespread.

compounded by the psychological trauma of confinement on reservations. Members of tribes that formerly hunted for their livelihoods, suddenly faced with restrictions on their movement and the inability to support themselves, passed their days idly. Many became depressed and turned to alcohol for solace. It did not help matters that Indians were pressured by the government to abandon old customs. Agents discouraged the practice of native religions and banned many types of ceremonies. They also contributed to the breakdown of Indian political systems by refusing to acknowledge the authority of tribal leaders. The BIA did try to help tribes become more self-sufficient and thus regain their dignity by providing training in European agricultural techniques and mechanical skills. But most Indians resisted such efforts, convinced that the white man's sedentary way of life was inferior to their own nomadic tradition.

The BIA had greater success with Indian schools. By the 1850s, the BIA funded more than 40 reservation schools operated by religious groups such as the American Missionary Association, the Bureau of Indian Missions, and the Mennonite Church. These schools were of various types. Some were day schools; others were boarding schools. Some offered a curriculum similar to that of schools for the general population; others provided vocational training. All of the schools were coeducational. In 1860, the BIA itself began operating schools on reservations. Between 1860 and 1870, the bureau established schools for the Yakima tribe in Washington, the Chippewa in Minnesota, and the Sauk and Fox in Oklahoma. These three schools, which all required their students to live on the premises, offered courses of study similar to the extremely rigorous programs of the religious schools. The BIA's annual report described a typical day at a mission school as follows: "Rise at half-past four; prayers at half-past five; work from breakfast to half-past eight; school at nine; dinner at twelve; school at half-past one; work from half-past four to six; prayers at eight, then immediately to bed."

Military Versus Civil Policy

During the 1850s and 1860s, as BIA agents offered aid to Indians on reservations, the U.S. Army continued to fight many of the tribes that remained at large. Underlying these contradictory civil and military policies were different attitudes toward Indians. One viewpoint held that Indians were born equal to whites and that they deserved to be treated with as much respect and to receive the same legal protection. This attitude had been championed for years by Christian missionaries. The opposing viewpoint maintained that

A sketch by artist Frederic Remington shows the Oglala Sioux performing the ghost dance. During the second half of the 19th century, BIA agents banned many Indian religious ceremonies.

Indians were innately inferior to whites and were incapable of adjusting to the modern world. Most BIA officials tended to hold the former view and saw as their goal the improvement of Indian welfare. Army leaders, by contrast, were dedicated to the annihilation of Indian tribes.

The wide disparity between civil and military policies often led to administrative conflict. In theory, military policy was supposed to operate in times of war, and civil policy in times of peace. But it was often hard to keep the BIA and the army confined to their appointed realms. Although BIA officials sought to eliminate army officials from treaty negotiations, some military officials finagled appointments as Indian agents. During the second half of the 19th century, officials developed several plans for reducing this conflict. For a time, Congress considered reincorporating the BIA into the War Department. George Manypenny, commissioner of Indian affairs from 1853 to 1857, proposed that the BIA form its own military force to assume the army's responsibility for military policy. Ultimately, both of these ideas were rejected.

Corruption and Reform

Not all agents took seriously the BIA's mandate to improve the welfare of the Indians. In fact, many used their positions to amass small fortunes, appropriating for themselves funds meant to be distributed among the Indians. By the mid-1860s, it was common knowledge that an agent could make enough money in a mere five years to retire—despite the position's relatively low salary of $2,000. For this reason, agency appointments were often distributed by presidents as rewards for political loyalty. Even agents who were sincere about helping Indians often had trouble understanding their needs, emphasizing religious education and agricultural training when basic economic assistance, coupled with tolerance for Indian traditions, would probably have been more helpful. Many agencies were also plagued by inefficiency and mismanagement.

During the Civil War, several religious and secular leaders, including Pierre Jean de Smet, John Beeson, and Bishop Henry B. Whipple, became concerned about the spread of corruption in the BIA and the increasing impoverishment of the Indians. At their request, Congress in 1865 agreed to appoint a joint House/Senate committee to examine Indian policy and consider reforms. Two years later, the committee published the results of its investigation, reporting that "many agents, teachers, and employees of the government are inefficient, faithless, and even guilty of peculations [embezzlement] and fraudulent practices upon the government and upon the Indians." The committee made

When Ulysses S. Grant took office as president in 1869, the BIA was plagued by corruption and mismanagement. During his presidency, Grant instituted several reforms, including the establishment of an oversight board to combat embezzlement of federal funds by BIA agents.

three other major observations: the Indian population was dwindling at an alarming rate, the majority of Indian wars were caused by the aggression of whites, and the Indians' impoverished condition could be attributed largely to the loss of their hunting grounds. The Indian Peace Commission, in its 1867 report, made similar findings: "The records are abundant to show that agents have pocketed the funds appropriated by the government and driven the Indians to starvation." The commission concluded that corruption and administrative weakness were to blame for several conflicts between the federal government and Indians, including the uprising of the Minnesota Sioux in 1862.

In 1869, Ulysses S. Grant took office as president, determined to carry out reforms in Indian policy. In a matter of months, Grant convinced Congress to set up a 10-member panel called the Board of Indian Commissioners. Initially charged with monitoring BIA finances, the board eventually became responsible for advising the secretary of the interior on all facets of Indian policy (a function that it served until 1933, when it was disbanded by President Franklin D. Roosevelt). Grant also took steps to eliminate the hiring of agents for political reasons, delegating authority for nominating new agents to religious organizations. By 1871, 67 of 74 Indian agencies were headed by officials nominated by religious groups. Although in the eyes of Grant's contemporaries, his reforms seemed radical, they were actually intended only to improve the administration of Indian affairs, not to change the overall direction of Indian policy.

Expansion of BIA Activities, 1870–1890

Agents appointed by religious groups took a greater interest than previous agents had in improving the welfare of Indians. Under their influence, between 1870 and 1890 the BIA significantly increased services for reservation Indians in such areas as law enforcement, education, health, and land development. In the process, agents and their staffs gradually became governments in miniature, supplying services that non-Indians received from federal, state, and local governments.

The general goal of the new agents was to turn reservations into "schools for civilization." To accomplish this goal, they felt that the BIA had to increase its control over reservations and reduce the influence of the army. In 1878, the BIA set up a tribal police force to take over the army's responsibility for preventing, investigating, and trying crimes on reservations. Within 6 years, the U.S. Indian Police was in operation on 48 of 60 existing reservations. Its

A tribal court in session on a South Dakota reservation. Under the influence of Christian missionaries, who filled the majority of agent positions during Grant's presidency, the BIA greatly expanded its judiciary and law-enforcement services on reservations.

staff numbered 162 officers and 653 privates and consisted entirely of whites—although it would later open its ranks to Indians. In its first years, the force had almost unlimited power to mete out punishment on the reservation. On several occasions, it ordered Indian criminals to be executed. But in the Major Crimes Act of 1885, Congress removed seven crimes—murder, manslaughter, rape, assault with intent to kill, arson, burglary, and larceny—from the jurisdiction of the Indian police and made them federal crimes that had to be tried in federal courts.

Education played an extremely important role in the effort by reform-minded BIA agents to "civilize" the Indians. Between 1870 and 1887, the BIA's budget for education increased from $100,000 to $1.2 million. By 1887, there were 227 Indian schools, 163 operated by the BIA and 64 run by religious groups. During this period, BIA officials decided that day schools and boarding schools on the reservation did not adequately isolate Indian youths from the influence of traditional ways. In the words of one agent, "On the reservation no school can be so conducted as to remove children from the influence of the idle and vicious who are everywhere present." The only way to avoid such influences, they decided, was to send Indian children to distant boarding schools. The

Sioux Indian boys pose for a photograph upon arriving at Carlisle Indian School in Pennsylvania, one of four off-reservation boarding schools set up for Indians by the BIA between 1879 and 1885. By 1887, the BIA operated a total of 163 schools.

bureau first experimented with the idea in 1878, sending 17 Indian students to Hampton Normal and Agricultural Institute (Hampton Institute), a boarding school in Virginia for the children of freed slaves. Then in 1879 the BIA founded the Carlisle Indian School in Pennsylvania, the first off-reservation school exclusively for Indians. During the following five years, three additional boarding schools were established: the Chemewa Indian School in Oregon, the Haskell Institute in Kansas, and the Chiloco Indian School in Oklahoma. In spite of the rapid expansion of the BIA educational system, Indian schools had only limited success. Their effectiveness was undercut by three major factors: the use of force to bring reluctant students to school; excessive punishment for infractions of trivial rules (such as the restriction against speaking Indian languages); and the intolerant attitude of white teachers toward Indian religions and values.

The BIA also expanded its health services during the 1870s and 1880s, in an effort to cope with the continuing problem of Indian vulnerability to the diseases of the white man. Doctors were stationed on most reservations, although facilities were often primitive. The first hospital for Indians was built in 1882 on the campus of the Carlisle Indian School.

At the same time, the BIA launched its first land development programs. The first attempt to help Indians irrigate their land was made in 1876 on the Colorado River Reservation in Arizona. On other reservations, the BIA helped hunting tribes use their land for livestock grazing.

The Last Indian Wars

Meanwhile, during the mid-1870s war had again broken out on the Plains. In 1874, army troops led by Colonel George Armstrong Custer discovered gold in the Black Hills of South Dakota, an area allotted to the Sioux by the 1868 Fort Laramie Treaty. After miners rushed into the area and refused a government order to leave, federal officials tried to purchase the Black Hills. When the Indians refused to sell, the government attempted to move the Indians off the land. Several bands of Northern Cheyenne and Oglala Sioux, under the command of the warrior Crazy Horse, resisted the plan and hostilities broke out.

On June 25, 1876, Crazy Horse and Sitting Bull, a Teton Sioux chief, led the Indians to their last and greatest victory, wiping out federal troops totaling 225 men, including Colonel Custer, at the Little Bighorn River. Attracting national attention, the massacre prompted federal officials to send in massive reinforce-

Indian youths ponder math problems at the Carlisle Indian School. The BIA established Indian boarding schools in order to isolate Indian youths as much as possible from the influence of traditional ways.

ments. The fresh troops were gradually able to round up the rebellious chiefs and their bands and move them onto reservations. Crazy Horse's Oglalas fought on the longest but in 1877, faced with starvation, they surrendered. Sitting Bull escaped to Canada but returned peacefully in 1881 and joined Buffalo Bill's Wild West Show.

In 1888, a last desperate movement to defeat the white man began. A Nevadan Indian named Wovoka had a vision in which the Indians again became dominant in North America by performing a ceremony called the ghost dance.

Within two years, Wovoka convinced several Plains tribes to take up the ghost dance. Concerned about an Indian uprising, BIA agents in South Dakota prohibited the ritual. When Sitting Bull protested the decision, a fight broke out and the renowned Indian leader was shot and killed. Appalled by the murder of their chief, several hundred Sioux held a demonstration at the town of Wounded Knee, South Dakota, near the Pine Ridge agency. BIA officials thought the Indians might be armed and ordered a squad of new recruits to surround and guard the assemblage. After several tense hours of waiting, one of the young recruits fired his gun. Within minutes hundreds of Indian men, women, and children had been brutally massacred. It was the last—and to the Indians the most horrible—of the conflicts.

By 1890, the Indian population had dwindled to about 300,000. The Indians' land base had shrunk to around 140 million acres. In spite of BIA efforts, most tribes continued to live in abject poverty. Indian traditions had been systematically wiped out. From the beginning of removal policy to the slaughter at Wounded Knee, the history of the Indians in the 19th century had truly been a "Trail of Tears."

Two aged Seminole Indians cast their ballots in an election held during the 1950s to determine whether their tribe would set up its own government. Over the course of the 20th century, the BIA has transferred many of its duties to tribal governments.

FOUR

The Road to Self-determination

In addition to expanding government services on reservations, during the 1870s and 1880s BIA agents promoted the concept of individual land ownership among Indians. By 1885, about 11,000 Indians owned their own farm plots on reservations. Giving Indians their own land and teaching them how to be farmers, BIA officials thought, was the best way to encourage them to assimilate into white society. And, in their view, assimilation was the only means by which Indians would be able to obtain rights and opportunities equal to those enjoyed by whites. The bureau was supported in this view by numerous self-proclaimed "friends of the Indian"—missionary leaders, members of Indian rights organizations, newspaper editors, and educational leaders. These advocates of Indian reform argued that reservations should function only as temporary way stations, places for Indians to receive education and other tools for survival before heading out into the surrounding society. Eventually, they insisted, as Indians assimilated reservations would disappear.

During the 1870s and 1880s, the BIA gave thousands of Indians—including this Arapaho family—their own farms as a way of promoting assimilation. In 1887, passage of the General Allotment Act made this practice the basis of federal Indian policy.

Land Allotment

In the 1880s, supporters of reform encouraged Congress to make assimilation through individual land ownership the primary goal of Indian policy. In 1887, Congress granted their wishes, enacting the General Allotment Act, also known as the Dawes Severalty Act. (Groups less sympathetic to the Indians had also supported land allotment as a way of reducing the Indians' share of the national territory. In the opinion of these groups, too much land had been reserved for what they saw as a "vanishing race.") Under the bill, a number of reservations were subdivided into tracts of 40, 80, and 160 acres, which were allotted to individual Indians. To prevent Indians from selling their new homesteads, actual ownership was not transferred immediately but instead was to be held in trust by the federal government for 25 years. But surplus land—land not allotted to individuals—was made available for purchase by non-Indians. The proceeds from the sales were placed in trust and used by the BIA to buy supplies for Indians.

Along with land allotment, the federal government took several other steps in attempting to bring about the assimilation of Indians. More Indian schools were built. A concerted effort was made to force Indians to give up their traditional dress, to abandon traditional religious practices, and to surrender their tribal loyalties. And, to reduce the power of Indian leaders, the BIA assumed additional governmental functions. In its 1888 report, the Board of Indian Commissioners praised the new policy: "The day when it was approved by the president may be called the Indians' emancipation day. It gives the Indian the possibility to become a man instead of remaining a ward of the government. It affords to him the opportunity to make for himself and his family a home, and to live among his equals a manly and independent life."

But as it turned out, the allotment policy had a devastating effect on Indians. Few Indians ever farmed their allotments. Many refused to become farmers because they considered such work unsuitable for men. Others wished to cultivate their plots but lacked sufficient funds and equipment to do so. During the 1890s, Congress passed a series of amendments to the Allotment Act that gave Indians the right to lease their land to non-Indians. Then, in 1906, the Burke Act gave Indians who were judged competent by the secretary of the interior the right to sell their land immediately—although the 25-year trust

Homesteaders and speculators rush to claim property on the Cherokee reservation, which the BIA opened up to settlement by non-Indians under the Allotment Act. During the allotment period, which lasted from 1887 to 1934, Indians lost 60 percent of their land.

period had not yet expired. Thousands of Indians took advantage of this ruling, selling their allotments to non-Indians who had the financial means and agricultural know-how to develop the land. Not accustomed to American money values and confused by the concept of individual land ownership, many Indians sold their land for much less than it was worth. After quickly exhausting the funds from the sale of their lands, most Indians had to turn again to the federal government for assistance. Consequently, allotment policy ultimately increased Indian dependence on the government—just the opposite of what it was intended to accomplish. Relatively few Indians actually assimilated into American society. Furthermore, the policy resulted in a massive transfer of land from Indians to whites: Between 1887 and 1934, Indian land holdings shrank from 138 million acres to 48 million acres. Several tribes actually became minorities on their own reservations. In the final analysis, allotment policy was a disaster for both Indians and the federal government.

The BIA's Role in Allotment

The BIA was responsible for implementing the allotment program. Its first task was to draw up a comprehensive list of the members of each tribe. To do this, the bureau had to develop criteria for deciding who was an Indian—in other words, how much Indian blood a person needed in order to be considered a member of a tribe. BIA staff members reviewed 250,000 applications for membership and accepted 101,000. The bureau's other primary tasks were to assess the value of Indian land, divide the land into individual farms, and help allottees settle the plots. In the process, agents also had to survey more than 300 towns, evict trespassers, sell surplus land, and administer the proceeds from the sales. As a result of these new duties, the number of BIA employees swelled from 1,725 in 1888 to 6,000 in 1911.

Under the General Allotment Act and later allotment bills passed by Congress, the BIA assumed the role of trustee for Indian lands and resources, a role it still fulfills today. The legal basis for the indefinite continuation of this role was the 1906 Burke Act, which authorized the bureau to extend its trusteeship beyond the 25-year deadline in situations where Indians were not yet deemed competent to sell their land. In its new role, the BIA launched several new programs to develop Indian land and natural resources. By 1920, appropriations for irrigation of Indian lands had increased markedly. In addition, land conservation and forestry projects had begun.

During the early 20th century, the BIA underwent a significant structural change. On the orders of Commissioner of Indian Affairs Francis E. Leupp, the bureau replaced many of its agents with school superintendents and farmers. The logic behind the move was that because several reservations had been divided up, the bureau's primary contact with many Indians was through education and agricultural training programs. Indians unaffiliated with reservations were assigned in small groups to a day-school teacher or farmer, who received instructions directly from the commisioner of Indian affairs.

Yet because the majority of reservations remained intact—although diminished in size—many agents retained their posts, performing the same functions as before. According to BIA historian Laurence Schmeckebeier, BIA functions in the early 20th century included: "allotting land; supervising the sale and leasing of land; custody of Indian money, both tribal and individual; education; furnishing medical relief; promoting industrial advancement, including the construction of irrigation, water supply, and drainage systems; the promotion of agriculture and stock raising, and the obtaining of employment; promoting home economics; policing reservations and punishing offenses; suppressing liquor traffic; and controlling Indian traders." By 1927, the year of Schmeckebeier's report, the overall structure of the department was fairly complex. The bureau consisted of the following: the commissioner of Indian affairs;

Osage leaders meet with Commissioner of Indian Affairs Cato Sells (seated, center) to discuss the extraction of oil from land on their reservation. During the early 1900s, the BIA gained increasing authority for managing Indian land and natural resources.

Indian children recover from tuberculosis at an Arizona sanitarium. To fight the spread of disease on Indian reservations, Congress, at the urging of President William Howard Taft, began appropriating funds for Indian medical services in 1911.

Medical Division; Purchase Division; Probate Division; Finance Division; Land Division; Irrigation Division; Forestry Division; Inspection Division; and Administrative Division.

During the early 20th century, the BIA was often charged with abusing its land allotment authority. For example, in 1909 a government investigation revealed that the BIA agent responsible for making allotments on the White Earth Chippewa reservation in Minnesota had given preferential treatment to tribal members with low proportions of Indian blood, assigning them the most valuable land. The mixed-blood allottees later sold their land to non-Indians under very suspicious circumstances. On many occasions, the BIA also abused its responsibility as trustee for Indian lands and resources. Between 1902 and

1908, for instance, the BIA authorized 22,000 leases for non-Indians on Indian land in Oklahoma—without allowing Indians a say in the decision or a significant share of the profits. The Bureau also pressured members of the Five Civilized Tribes (the Creek, Cherokee, Choctaw, Chickasaw, and Seminole tribes) to sell mineral-rich land in the former Indian Territory.

Victimized by corruption and alienated from their land, American Indians entered the second decade of the 20th century in a desperate condition. The allotment policy had done little to bring Indians into the mainstream of American society. Poverty continued to be widespread. Particularly distressing on reservations was the prevalence of two wretched diseases—tuberculosis and trachoma (an inflammation of the inner surface of the eyelids). Health conditions began to improve in 1911, however, when President William Howard Taft received a BIA report on the Indian health crisis and immediately resolved to seek improved medical services on reservations. Taft soon convinced Congress to appropriate $40,000 for Indian medical services. More important, the president's interest in the issue aroused the concern of the American public about the shameful conditions that existed on reservations. In response to the report, the Public Health Service conducted a survey of Indian health. Its final report helped convince Congress to increase outlays for Indian medical services to $350,000 by 1918.

The Meriam Report

Congress improved the administration of Indian affairs in the 1921 Snyder Act, which clarified the BIA's duties in light of its increased governmental functions on reservations. And legislators passed the Indian Citizenship Act in 1924, granting Indians U.S. citizenship and the right to vote in local, state, and national elections. (Some Indians had been granted citizenship by treaties as early as 1817. In 1919, Indians who had enlisted in the armed forces during World War I were awarded citizenship, but universal citizenship did not become law until 1924.) Still, many public officials and Indian rights groups— such as the American Indian Defense Association, the Indian Rights Organization, and the Indian Welfare Committee of the General Federation of Womens' Clubs—felt that federal Indian policy was in dire need of reform.

In response to public pressure, in 1926 the secretary of the interior commissioned a private research organization, the Institute for Government Research, to make a thorough investigation of the BIA. In 1928, the institute issued its final report, which was edited by Lewis Meriam and entitled *Problems of Indian Administration*. The Meriam Report, as it became known, recommended several changes in BIA policy. It called for changes in personnel practices—better salaries for all employees and the hiring of more Indian staff members. The report also urged increased appropriations for health and education. It recommended the de-emphasis of boarding schools in favor of day schools, where Indian students could be in closer contact with their tribes. And it recommended that the BIA establish a Division of Planning "to hasten agricultural advances, vocational guidance, job placement, and other aspects of economic development." Regarding the allotment program, the Meriam Report charged that the government had ensured its failure by not paying adequate attention to instructing Indians in agricultural techniques. "It almost seems as if the government assumed that some magic in individual ownership of property would in itself prove an educational, civilizing factor." The report also recommended the termination of allotment.

Pueblo Indians from New Mexico arrive in Washington, D.C., in 1923 to lobby against a bill that would reduce Indian land holdings in the southwest. The furor over the bill increased support for reforms in Indian policy.

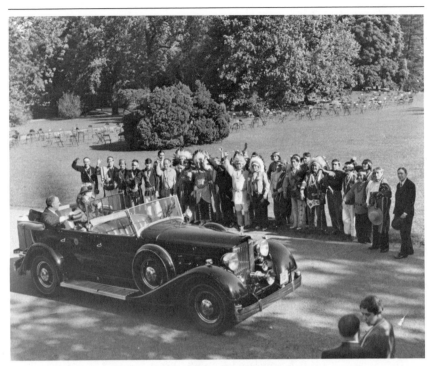

At the behest of President Franklin D. Roosevelt, pictured here touring the Navajo reservation, in 1934 Congress passed the Indian Reorganization Act. The act ended the allotment of Indian land and authorized tribes to establish their own governments.

Indian Reorganization Act

Most of the recommendations in the Meriam Report were later incorporated into the Indian Reorganization Act (Wheeler-Howard Act), passed by Congress in 1934. The product of lobbying by John Collier, President Franklin D. Roosevelt's energetic commissioner of Indian affairs, the act represented a significant departure in Indian policy. It ended the process of allotment, banned the unregulated sale of Indian lands, and authorized appropriations to purchase new lands for tribes. It directed the secretary of the interior to draw up regulations, based on modern conservation principles, to govern logging and rangeland grazing. It also provided for a system of federal loans for tribal economic development. But the most important part of the law established procedures by which tribes could organize their own governments. Tribes

73

Portrait of an Indian Commissioner:
John Collier

Since the establishment of the Bureau of Indian Affairs, more than 40 men have served as commissioner of Indian affairs, including distinguished lawyers, former congressmen, gentlemen farmers, Indians, Indian fighters, scholars, and career bureaucrats. None has been more effective or energetic than John Collier, a social worker and Indian-rights activist who was appointed head of the BIA by President Franklin D. Roosevelt in 1933. Collier brought to his position a deep concern for the disinherited and a commitment to progressive reform. During his 12 years in office—the longest tenure of any Indian affairs commissioner—Collier fought to preserve traditional tribal culture and Indian lands, both of which had been threatened under the federal policy of allotment. While Roosevelt launched a group of public works projects known as the New Deal, Collier set in motion the "Indian New Deal," a slate of reforms that improved economic conditions on reservations and for the first time gave Indians a voice in their own affairs. His efforts culminated in the Indian Reorganization Act, which ended the dismantling of reservations, authorized tribes to set up their own government, and appropriated funds to help them establish business ventures.

Born in Atlanta, Georgia, on May 4, 1884, into an elite southern family, Collier received a broad but haphazard education, studying literature at Columbia University in New York,

attending psychology classes at the Collège de France in Paris, and learning about social work from Lucy Graham Crozier, a private teacher. At Crozier's insistence, in 1907 Collier accepted a job at the People's Institute, a social-work organization that attempted to provide New York's immigrant population with a sense of community. Over the next several years, Collier became involved in several projects on Manhattan's Lower East Side. He set up a training school for community workers and spearheaded a movement to turn public schools into community centers. In the process, he became convinced that immigrants could cope most effectively with the pressures of industrial society by preserving old-world social structures and customs. (He would later apply this theory to Indians as well.)

After World War I, Collier moved to California, where he directed that state's adult education program and taught political theory and history. In the winter of 1920, Mabel Dodge, whose Greenwich Village salons Collier had frequently attended, convinced him to visit the Taos Indian Pueblo in New Mexico. It was a revelation. Deciding that the village was a utopian (ideal) community that possessed "the secret of human life," Collier resolved to launch a crusade on behalf of American Indians. In 1923, he helped found the American Indian Defense Association, an Indian-rights lobbying group located in Washington, D.C. As executive secretary of the association

John Collier, commissioner of Indian affairs from 1933 to 1945, meets with Indian representatives in Washington, D.C.

from 1923 to 1933, Collier worked to improve the welfare of native Americans. Soon after taking office, he helped defeat the Barsum Bill, a measure that would have significantly reduced Pueblo Indian land holdings by requiring Indians to prove the lands were legally theirs.

Throughout the 1920s, Collier criticized the BIA for its failure to protect resources and for its antagonism to traditional Indian customs—particularly religious ceremonies. Ultimately, Collier's accusations prompted the secretary of the interior to ask the Institute for Government Research (Brookings Institution), a private organization, to conduct an investigation of the BIA.

In 1933, President Roosevelt selected Collier as his commissioner of Indian affairs. Within two years, Collier and his staff had steered through Congress four major bills: the Pueblo Relief Bill (1933), which compensated Indians at the Rio Grande Pueblo for land taken by non-Indian settlers; the Johnson-O'Malley Act (1934), which appropriated federal funds to state governments to expand health, education, and social welfare services; the Indian Reorganization Act (1934); and a bill that established an Indian Arts and Crafts Board. Collier also carried out significant reforms in the area of Indian education. He closed down boarding schools, ordered the construction of several day schools with funds from the Public Works Administration, instituted a progressive curriculum that stressed skills needed for rural living, and introduced the first bilingual education program for Indians. Collier's other major accomplishments included increasing the number of Indian employees in the BIA from 30 to 65 percent, reforming the Indian court system, and obtaining $100 million from New Deal relief and recovery agencies for the benefit of Indians.

Collier retired from government service in 1945 and until his death in 1968 continued to fight for Indian rights. In 1964, the Department of the Interior awarded him its Distinguished Service Award, recognizing that his career as BIA commissioner "brought hope of a better day and a brighter future to a whole people."

Johnston Murray, the first Indian governor of Oklahoma, dines with an Indian chief and his wife at the BIA's Concho Indian School in 1951. During the 1950s, the goal of Indian policy was to terminate the federal government's responsibility for Indian tribes.

were also authorized to incorporate, or legally organize (in the same way that American towns and cities incorporate), for the purpose of launching business enterprises such as utility companies and tourist industries. Incorporated tribes were eligible to receive loans for economic development. Under the Indian Reorganization Act, the essence of Indian policy became "cooperation between Indian tribes and the federal government to achieve change without forcing it," in the words of one historian. Commissioner Collier saw it this way: "The bill is the beginning in the process of liberating and rejuvenating a subjugated and exploited race living in the midst of an aggressive civilization far ahead, materially speaking."

In the two years following the passage of the Indian Reorganization Act, a series of Indian congresses were held across the United States in which Indian tribes were allowed to choose whether or not the act would apply to them. Ultimately, 181 tribal groups accepted the plan and 77 rejected it. Those who

76

accepted it proceeded to form governments based on tribal councils and governed by new constitutions.

The Indian Reorganization Act markedly enhanced the economic standing of most tribes. Following the bill's passage, Indian agricultural production, particularly of beef and corn, increased enormously. At the same time, Indian tourist enterprises proliferated across the country, especially in the Southwest, and brought in much-needed cash revenue. The improved economic health of Indian tribes was evidenced by the repayment of almost all federal loans made during this period within 10 years.

Two other bills passed by Congress during the 1930s further improved the lives of Indians. Under the Johnson-O'Malley Act of 1934, Congress authorized the BIA to arrange with state governments for the provision of educational, social, and health services to supplement federal services. In 1935, Congress created the Indian Arts and Crafts Board within the Department of the Interior. The new board helped Indians to revive native arts and crafts and to sell these objects to tourists and collectors.

A Reversal: Reduction of Federal Responsibility

In the 1940s and 1950s, the federal government changed its Indian policy, seeking ways to reduce and ultimately terminate the federal role in Indian affairs, particularly the BIA's responsibility as a trustee of Indian lands and resources. In 1943, the United States Senate had conducted yet another survey of Indian conditions and once again found serious problems. The Bureau of Indian Affairs and federal bureaucracy were held responsible.

House Concurrent Resolution 108 in 1953 established termination of federal responsibility as the basis for Indian policy. It declared that "Indian tribes and individual members . . . should be freed from Federal supervision and control and from all disabilities and limitations specially applicable to Indians." The commissioner of Indian affairs developed criteria to identify tribal groups that could be removed from the federal trust relationship. Members of Congress took the position that some tribes were sufficiently acculturated and that for them the protective role of the Bureau of Indian Affairs was no longer needed. During the 1950s, the BIA aggressively pursued the termination of the trust relationship of specific tribes, the transfer of federal responsibility and jurisdiction to state governments, and the physical relocation of Indian people from reservations to urban areas. Between 1954 and 1962, specific legislation was passed authorizing the termination of BIA supervision of more than 100 tribes, bands, and Indian *rancherias* (social and political Indian communities in California).

Another Reversal: Indian Self-determination

In March 1968, President Lyndon B. Johnson sent a message on Indian affairs to Congress, proposing to "erase old attitudes of paternalism and promote partnership and self-help." President Johnson stated: "Our goal must be: A standard of living for Indians equal to that of the country as a whole, freedom of choice—an opportunity to remain in their homeland, if they choose, without surrendering their dignity, and an opportunity to move to the towns and cities of America if they choose, equipped with skills to live in equality and dignity; full participation in the life of modern America, with a full share of economic opportunity and social justice."

Johnson's message, the first clear enunciation of federal Indian policy since 1953, officially ended the "termination" effort begun during the 1950s. Soon afterward, Johnson established the National Council on Indian Opportunity to make a thorough investigation of federal programs for Indians and to promote Indian participation in decision-making. Chaired by the vice president, the council included both federal officials and Indian leaders.

Richard M. Nixon, who became president in 1969, maintained Johnson's new Indian policy and further clarified its goals. In a special message to Congress on July 8, 1970, Nixon asserted that "It is long past time that the Indian policies of the federal government began to . . . build upon the capacities and insights of the Indian people." He proposed a policy based on three premises: (1) the federal government's trust responsibility and its provision of reservation services would not be terminated without Indian consent; (2) tribal governments would be given the option of taking over operation of federally funded programs; (3) tribes would be encouraged to become economically self-sufficient. The new policy, which remains in effect today, was termed self-determination.

In 1969, the BIA was significantly reorganized under Nixon's commissioner of Indian affairs, Louis Bruce, an Indian of Sioux-Mohawk descent. Bruce, only the third Indian ever to head the BIA, realigned the agency's structure and formed a new executive staff, consisting of 14 Indians, 1 Eskimo, and 4 non-Indians (more Indians than had ever before held BIA management

Under President Lyndon B. Johnson, the BIA abandoned the policy of "termination" and instituted a new policy known as self-determination, under which tribes were given the choice of continuing to receive federal services or providing those services themselves.

A car carrying the assistant attorney general is escorted through Wounded Knee, South Dakota, by armed members of the American Indian Movement (AIM) during the militant group's 1973 occupation of the historic town.

positions). In 1970, the BIA was placed in charge of implementing self-determination policy. In May, Commissioner Bruce announced five goals to guide the bureau in its new direction:

• Transformation of the BIA from a management to a service organization.

• Reaffirmation of the trust status of Indian land.

• Making the Bureau of Indian Affairs' area offices responsive to the Indian people they serve.

• Providing tribes with the option of taking over any or all BIA program functions with the understanding that the bureau would provide assistance or reassume control if requested to do so.

• Working with Indian rights organizations to become a strong advocate of urban Indian interests.

In May 1970, the Zuni Indians became the first tribe to assume responsibility for federal programs. A year later, the Miccosukee tribe contracted with the BIA to provide all educational and social services on the tribe's reservation in Florida. The assumption of new responsibilities by these two tribes reflected an increasing optimism among Indians about being able to improve their lives through active involvement in their own affairs. During the late 1960s, this same feeling was also manifest in the proliferation of Indian rights organizations, including the National Tribal Chairmen's Association (NTCA), an association of tribal leaders set up to advise the BIA on behalf of reservation Indians. Two other organizations, the National Congress of American Indians and the American Indian Movement (AIM), were formed to voice the concerns of Indians living in urban areas.

Indian activists often engaged in acts of civil disobedience to press their demands. Beginning in 1969, Indians on several occasions occupied surplus federal land, demanding that the federal government relinquish some of the territory that had been unfairly taken from Indians over the years. In October 1969, a group of Indians took over Alcatraz Island, a former prison in San Francisco Bay. Nineteen months later, the Indians agreed to end the occupation under the condition that the government establish an Indian culture center on the island. A year later, however, federal officials made Alcatraz an historic prison exhibit as part of the Golden Gate National Recreation Area. In 1971, similar occupations took place in Chicago—where Indians took over a missile site to demand more affordable housing—and Mount Rushmore— where Indians camped out for several weeks demanding that the federal government honor the 1869 Sioux Treaty of Fort Laramie by returning all land in South Dakota west of the Missouri River. Partly in response to these occupations, President Nixon convinced Congress to restore 48,000 acres of land to the Taos Pueblo Indians of New Mexico. It was the first time the government had ever returned land taken from Indians. Before then, compensation had always been made in the form of cash payments.

The two most dramatic and highly publicized incidents involving Indian activists occurred later in the 1970s. In November 1972, members of a group called the Trail of Broken Treaties arrived in Washington, D.C., after traveling across the United States in a caravan that recalled the "Trail of Tears." On November 2, after an unproductive meeting with an assistant secretary of the interior, Harrison Loesch, the Indian group decided to occupy the BIA's headquarters. During a tumultuous 7-day occupation, many of the BIA's offices were ransacked, files were destroyed, and artwork was stolen. Ultimately,

A meeting of the Navajo tribal council. In 1975, under the Indian Self-determination and Education Assistance Act, Indian governments began contracting with the BIA to operate their own schools and provide other services on reservations.

however, Indian leaders were unsuccessful in their attempt to secure a meeting with President Nixon. Federal officials refused to consider the activists' demands until all stolen documents and artifacts were returned.

On February 27, 1973, nearly 200 members of the American Indian Movement (AIM) seized control of the historic town of Wounded Knee, South Dakota. Led by Russell Means, the activists called for reform of tribal governments, charging that tribal leaders who had gained control under the Indian Reorganization Act had abused their powers. But the demonstration ended 71 days later with no concrete gains.

In 1975, Congress passed the Indian Self-Determination and Education Assistance Act, which greatly increased the powers of tribal governments to contract with the BIA to provide services and programs for members. Under this bill, the BIA began transforming itself from a direct service agency to a contracting or granting agency.

On January 24, 1983, President Reagan, in an American Indian policy statement. reaffirmed the government-to-government relationship of Indian tribes with the United States, expanded the 1970 national policy of Indian self-determination, and requested special efforts to develop Indian reservation economies. With regard to earlier federal Indian policies, President Reagan said that they "have, by and large, inhibited the political and economic development of the tribes. Excessive regulation and self-perpetuating bureaucracy have stifled local decision-making, thwarted Indian control of Indian resources and promoted dependency rather than self-sufficiency. This administration intends to reverse this trend."

*A member of the Papago Indian tribal police. The BIA operates po-
lice departments on several reservations and oversees police departments organized by tribal governments.*

FIVE

The Bureau of Indian Affairs Today

The Bureau of Indian Affairs is not the only federal agency that provides services to Indians and executes federal Indian policy. But it has primary responsibility for this task. And it is the only federal agency that interacts with Indian tribes in a government-to-government manner, rather than dealing with Indians as individuals.

The BIA's many functions can be divided into four categories. First, the bureau ensures that all Indians have adequate educational opportunities. It operates 115 elementary schools, postsecondary schools, and colleges; provides funding to the 85 percent of Indian students who attend public and parochial schools; offers financial assistance to Indians attending college; and helps tribes set up their own schools. It also helps develop special educational programs such as vocational training and adult education.

Second, the bureau provides reservation Indians with services that non-Indians receive from local governments. Among these services are police protection, road construction and maintenance, welfare payments, funding for housing, job placement and training, and medical care for the disadvantaged.

Third, the bureau administers and manages 53 million acres of land held in trust by the United States for Indians. Reservations constitute most of this trust land, but not all reservation land is held in trust. As part of the trust responsibility, the BIA manages fish and wildlife resources on Indian lands, manages forests, leases mineral rights, manages water rights, oversees agricultural development, and directs conservation efforts. The bureau's trust responsibility evolved from a series of laws passed by Congress and has been voluminously interpreted by the courts; but it has never been explicitly defined in a single statute. Thus, disagreements often result over how far the trust relationship extends. During the 1950s, the government terminated its trust relationship with several tribes. The current policy, however, calls for existing tribal-government relationships to continue indefinitely.

Fourth, and most important, the bureau—in accordance with the current policy of self-determination—helps Indians assume as much responsibility as possible for their own affairs. Toward this end, the BIA assists tribes in establishing their own governments and acts as the intermediary between them and the federal government. The BIA also encourages tribal governments to take over services usually provided by the federal government, and the bureau supplies necessary funding and technical assistance to those that choose to do so. To promote economic self-sufficiency, the BIA helps Indian tribes establish and operate business enterprises, such as bingo halls, tourist hotels and restaurants, manufacturing concerns, mining companies, ski resorts, and museums. It makes business loans available and assists tribes in attracting outside investment.

Organizational Structure

The BIA is a division of the Department of the Interior (DOI). The bureau's highest official is not actually a BIA employee but rather is one of the five assistant secretaries of the DOI, the assistant secretary for Indian affairs. The position was created by President Jimmy Carter in 1977. Prior to that time, the BIA was headed by an official within the BIA, the commissioner of Indian affairs, and was represented in the DOI by an assistant secretary who was responsible for several other offices and bureaus and thus could not devote full attention to advocating BIA programs. The transfer of authority to the assistant secretary for Indian affairs has given the BIA greater visibility and influence within the DOI and with Congress. At present, the arrangement is considered an "acting" one; in other words, it has never been recognized in a statute. In theory, the position of commissioner of Indian affairs still exists, beneath the assistant secretary; but in practice it has been vacant since 1981. All four persons who have held the position of assistant secretary for Indian affairs have been Indians.

The staff of the assistant secretary for Indian affairs is divided into several departments: Congressional and Legislative Affairs, Equal Employment Opportunity, Correspondence, Facilities Engineering, Intergovernmental Relations, School Facilities, and Public Information. Subordinate to these divisions in the BIA chain of command are the bureau's four main offices: Indian Education, Administration, Indian Services, and Trust Responsibilities. Most employees of these offices work in the BIA's Washington, D.C., headquarters, but some are stationed in area offices or on reservations. In general, the responsibilities of the BIA's central office are to develop the BIA's policies, programs, and budgets; to draw up reports and proposals for legislation to be submitted to Congress; to serve as a liaison with other federal agencies with regard to Indian programs; and to supervise area and agency offices.

To implement BIA programs and policies on the local level, there are 11 area offices and 82 agencies. Most BIA employees work at these levels. (In 1988, 13,239 people worked for the BIA.) The area offices are located in Sacramento, California; Phoenix, Arizona; Window Rock, Arizona; Muskogee, Oklahoma; Anadarko, Oklahoma; Minneapolis, Minnesota; Juneau, Alaska; Billings, Montana; Albuquerque, New Mexico; Portland, Oregon; and Aberdeen, South Dakota. Three of the BIA's four main offices, Administration, Trust Responsibilities, and Indian Services, deal directly with area and agency offices, while the fourth, Indian Education, implements its programs through local school boards and regional educational offices. Many agencies utilize personnel from the main divisions. For instance, if an agency is located on a reservation that operates several irrigation projects, employees from the Office of Trust Responsibilities' Division of Water and Land Resources may be stationed there.

The Office of Indian Education

The Office of Indian Education is responsible for operating BIA schools and for overseeing and funding schools operated by various tribal governments. In 1987, the office funded 181 educational facilities. Of these, 57 day schools, 40 on-reservation boarding schools, 6 off-reservation boarding schools, and 9 dormitories were run by the education office itself. (The dormitories are operated by the BIA to facilitate public school attendance for Indian students.) Another 53 day schools, 10 on-reservation boarding schools, 1 off-reservation boarding school, and 5 dormitories were run by Indian tribes under contract with the education office. Total enrollment in BIA-funded schools in 1987 was 40,000.

Navajo Community College in Tsaile, Arizona, is 1 of 20 tribally operated community colleges for which the BIA's Education Office provides funds. The Education Office, which receives the largest budget allotment of any BIA division, operates three postsecondary institutions.

The BIA-operated schools are usually in isolated areas. Some are full-time boarding schools for children from areas where there is no school nearby, or for those with family, learning, or behavioral problems.

Under the Johnson-O'Malley Act, the education office also provides funds to meet the needs of Indian students attending public, private, and parochial schools. In 1987, there were 178,000 such students.

An increasing number of Indians are high-school graduates. In 1985, the Bureau of Indian Affairs awarded 16,000 college scholarships. The education office also provides grants for the operation of 20 tribally controlled community colleges. In 1987, there were 3,934 Indian students enrolled in these colleges. The BIA itself runs three postsecondary schools: Haskell Indian Junior College in Lawrence, Kansas; the Institute of American Indian Arts in Santa Fe, New Mexico; and the Southwestern Indian Polytechnic Institute in Albuquerque, New Mexico.

A Navajo Indian uses colored sand to make a ceremonial design. The BIA's Indian Arts and Crafts Board promotes the revitalization of native arts and crafts both to stimulate reservation economies and to preserve a rich cultural heritage.

A Zuni Indian fire fighter with a traditional decoration on his helmet. The BIA's Division of Self-Determination Services, part of the Office of Indian Services, helps tribal governments secure federal contracts to provide such services as fire protection on reservations.

Office of Indian Services

The Office of Indian Services receives the second-largest budget allotment and is responsible for a great variety of services.

The Division of Tribal Services provides funds and technical assistance to tribes to help improve their government operations and judicial capacities. It is also responsible for the research and processing of petitions submitted by unrecognized Indian groups that are seeking to be recognized by the federal government.

The Division of Social Services administers welfare assistance grants for Indians on or near reservations who cannot get assistance from local or state agencies. These grants are used for direct financial assistance to individual Indians and for funding Indian family service programs, such as counseling, day care, and employment training.

The Law Enforcement division provides police protection and detention services similar to those of police departments in non-Indian communities. It operates on 163 reservations.

The Division of Housing Services helps tribes obtain low-cost, federally financed housing from the Department of Housing and Urban Development or the Farmers Home Administration. When tribal members do not qualify for other federal programs, the Bureau of Indian Affairs provides low-cost loans to them for new homes or repairs to existing homes.

The Division of Self-Determination Services helps tribes contract with the government to administer reservation programs normally handled by the BIA. The division also provides grants to tribes to help them improve the management of federal programs.

The Economic Development and Employment Program promotes the employment and economic growth of Indian people. It provides adult vocational

A steam shovel digs up coal deposits on land that the Peabody Coal Company leases from the Navajo tribe. The BIA's Office of Trust Responsibilities is in charge of granting leases for mining, logging, farming, and other economic development on Indian trust lands.

and on-the-job training, work experience, and job placement programs.

Business, commercial, industrial, and tourism enterprises are promoted through the Business Enterprise Development Program. The BIA works with tribes to get private firms to locate on or near reservations. In recent years more than 250 manufacturing and commercial projects, providing more than 15,000 jobs, have been established with the assistance of the BIA. The BIA also makes business and economic development loans and assists tribes in obtaining financing from other sources.

The Indian Arts and Crafts Board promotes the development of Indian arts and crafts in order to improve the economy and preserve the heritage of the American Indians. The secretary of the interior appoints five commissioners to

A hygienist for the Indian Health Service (IHS), a division of the Department of Health and Human Services, shows Indian children the proper method for brushing their teeth. Of the federal agencies that supplement BIA services for Indians, the IHS is the most important.

this board. They serve without compensation and employ a professional staff. This staff operates three regional museums: the Sioux Indian Museum in Rapid City, South Dakota; the Museum of the Plains Indian in Browning, Montana; and the Southern Plains Indian Museum in Anadarko, Oklahoma.

There are 83 Indian agencies that have natural resource programs. Through the Natural Resources Development program, the BIA encourages the use of the 53 million acres of Indian land to their full potential. It promotes sound conservation practices in order to protect the resources while making them productive so that they supply income to the tribes that own them. It assists tribes in developing and managing water, forestry, fish, wildlife, and mineral resources and constructs, operates, and maintains irrigation projects on Indian lands.

Office of Trust Responsibilities

The Office of Trust Responsibilities protects Indian lands. Every aspect of land ownership, land acquisition or disposal, land use, and resources connected with land fall under the trust responsibility. Any inadequate exercise of the trust responsibility by the federal government potentially subjects the government to legal action for damages. The secretary of the interior is legally responsible for the Indians' land so long as it is held in trust by the federal government for the American Indians.

Interactions with Other Government Agencies

The BIA works with other bureaus in the Department of the Interior that provide services to American Indians. The United States Geological Survey performs inspections, reviews permits and lease plans, and develops environmental impact assessments for oil, gas, and coal extraction on Indian reservations. The U.S. Fish and Wildlife Service gives technical assistance to tribes in the preparation of fish-management plans, especially fish-hatchery and fish-stocking programs on the reservations. In the 1980s, the Bureau of Reclamation began building the waterworks for an irrigation project on the Navajo reservation. These are just some of the services made available from other bureau programs to American Indians with the assistance of the BIA.

There are also other agencies and offices in the federal government that have programs relating specifically to American Indians. The Department of

Economic Development on Indian Reservations:
Ski Resorts and Bingo Halls

During the 1930s, the federal government began subsidizing economic development on Indian reservations in an effort to combat widespread poverty. Under the 1934 Indian Reorganization Act, the BIA provided loans and technical assistance to tribal governments seeking to establish independent business enterprises. For several years, these efforts focused on logging and farming. Then, during the 1960s, as Indian unemployment rates soared, reservations became a primary target of President Lyndon B. Johnson's War on Poverty. Set in motion by several government agencies—including the BIA, the Department of Labor, and the Office of Economic Opportunity—Johnson's programs emphasized training Indians to work in urban areas outside the reservations.

In 1972, under Commissioner Louis R. Bruce, the BIA abandoned this policy and dedicated itself to developing businesses on reservations. Through its Business Enterprise Development Division, the BIA encouraged tribes to launch projects in manufacturing, tourism, communications, and finance. Between 1972 and 1984, the number of businesses on reservations increased from 110 to 260.

Today, many tribes run businesses on their reservations. In cooperation with the Brunswick Corporation, the Devils Lake Sioux tribe in North Dakota operates a factory that manufactures camouflage clothing. The Mississippi Choc-

taw own 100 percent of a company called the Chahta Enterprise, which manufactures wiring units for automobiles. The Mescalero Apache own Sierra Blanco, a popular ski resort in the southern Rocky Mountains. Many tribes receive substantial income from farming, ranching, and logging projects. In 1980, the total value of products grown on Indian land was more than $1 billion. Other tribes earn money by leasing the rights to minerals located beneath their reservation land. Fifteen tribes each make more than $1 million a year on oil and gas leases, including the Osage ($65 million),

A bingo hall on the Mashantucket Pequot Indian reservation in Connecticut.

94

the Navajo ($25 million), and the Wind River ($17 million).

No industry has been more profitable for Indians than bingo. Tribes began operating bingo halls during the late 1970s, when tribal leaders discovered that because reservations fell under federal jurisdiction, Indian bingo games would not be subject to prize money limits set by state governments. Thus, whereas non-Indian bingo establishments could offer a maximum payout of only $500, Indian casinos were free to offer virtually unlimited prize money, along with door prizes such as cars, boats, and vacations. Indian bingo halls soon became popular, especially in states where other forms of gambling were prohibited. By 1987, approximately 140 high-stakes bingo games had been established on reservations in 23 states. Operated by tribal governments, Indian bingo games have catered primarily to non-Indian customers.

Yet in spite of the proliferation of commercial enterprises on reservations, most Indian economies remain extremely depressed, with unemployment rates that rank among the highest in the nation. In part, Indian economic difficulties stem from the inability of most Indian companies to make a profit. For instance, the 12 biggest Indian tourism enterprises all lose money every year, according to a BIA-financed study. Those tribes that manage to stay in the black often find their economic development hindered by government bureaucracy. For instance, the Sauk and Fox tribe almost lost the opportunity to purchase Midwest Textiles because one of the BIA officials who had to approve the purchase went on vacation a month before the deal was to close. Said Jack Thorpe, the Sauk and Fox chief, "We've simply surpassed the ability of the BIA to deal with us. Many of the things we're doing as a tribe are beyond the BIA bureaucrats' technical knowledge and background to understand."

A task force created by President Ronald Reagan to study Indian development found several other reasons for the slow pace: "Reservations are often isolated, have poor-quality land, and have harsh climates. In many tribes individual entrepreneurship and the pursuit of private profit have not been a valued and encouraged form of behavior. Because of the lack of previous economic development, the labor force on many reservations is not highly trained and sometimes lacks the experience that would instill work habits sought by modern industry." Still, there is some cause for optimism. The creation of the task force indicates that the government has at least begun to acknowledge the problem. In addition, Congress is considering the establishment of an Indian Redevelopment Bank and the creation on reservations of enterprise zones, in which non-Indian companies would receive tax breaks for setting up businesses.

Housing and Urban Development has assisted tribes in obtaining new and improved housing. The Department of Health and Human Services provides services that range from social security to health care for Indians of all ages. The most important of these programs is the Indian Health Service, which is a bureau within the Health Services Administration of the Public Health Service. The Indian Health Service offers comprehensive health services for American Indians and Alaska natives. The Department of Education coordinates federal assistance to education programs. Most of the programs for Indians are under the jurisdiction of the assistant secretary for elementary and secondary education. The Office of Indian Education Programs administers grants to local education agencies in order to provide special educational and cultural programs for Indian children. This office also oversees the awarding of grants to improve educational opportunities for adult Indians.

Who Benefits?

According to the U.S. Census Bureau, in 1980 there were 1,418,195 Indians, Eskimos, and Aleuts in the United States. Approximately 700,000 of them belong to federally recognized tribes or communities. Only members of

An Indian rider surveys picturesque Monument Valley, which is situated on the Navajo Indian reservation, spanning the Utah-Arizona border. In 1987, about 300 of the 512 federally recognized tribes had their own reservations.

An Eskimo girl who attends a BIA school in Alaska. The BIA's service population includes not only Indians who live in the 48 contiguous states but also Eskimos, Aleuts, and Alaskan Indians.

officially recognized tribes are eligible for BIA services. Most of these Indians reside on or near reservations. The remaining Indians either belong to tribal groups that are not federally recognized or are people of Indian descent who have no tribal affiliation.

Recognized tribes have attained their status in the past in a number of ways—some by signing treaties with the U.S. government, some through executive order or presidential proclamation, and some through federal legislation. Unrecognized tribes are of several types—some never signed treaties with the U.S. government, some signed treaties for which records have been lost, some remained isolated from white men for most of history, and some enjoyed acknowledgment but were later "terminated" by Congress. Of the approximately 200 unacknowledged tribes, 45 have submitted recognition petitions to the BIA since 1972. They are seeking recognition for two main reasons: They have pride in their tribal heritage, and they hope to become eligible for federal programs.

Unaffiliated Indians may become members of a tribe in either of two ways: by satisfying membership criteria established by Congress or through adoption by a tribe. The percentage of Indian ancestry required for membership varies from tribe to tribe. For some tribes, only a trace of Indian blood is necessary, whereas for others as much as half is required.

In 1970, several hundred Indians occupied San Francisco's Alcatraz Island, formerly a federal prison, to press their demand that Indian land illegally obtained by the federal government be returned. One of the many challenges the BIA will face in the future is that of dealing with an increasingly powerful Indian rights movement.

SIX

A Controversial Past, An Uncertain Future

Each presidential administration has asked itself what to do with the American Indians. The answers, expressed in the twists and turns of Indian policy, have generated significant controversy. Extensive federal involvement in Indian affairs began in 1789, when the U.S. Constitution provided Congress with the exclusive right to regulate commerce with Indian tribes. In the succeeding years, federal Indian policy evolved as the government attempted to define the basic premises of the interaction between non-Indian people and Indians. The BIA gradually became a buffer and mediator between these two extremely diverse populations. In the process, the bureau was also frequently singled out as being the cause of the Indians' troubles.

Throughout the history of the United States, American Indians have been treated as a "problem" rather than as a people. The books in our public schools too often provided a one-sided account of how the Indians impeded progress, justice, and civilization. The Indians have been viewed as "savages" because they have tried to protect their way of life and their land. During the 19th century, most Americans believed that the Indians would eventually disappear, and with them "the Indian problem."

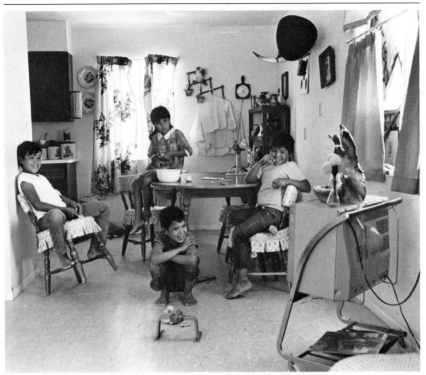

Navajo children watch television in their home in Kayenta, Arizona, a city on the Navajo reservation. For Indian children, the future is clouded by the continuing problems of the BIA—administrative inefficiency, mismanagement of Indian resources, and inability to understand Indians' needs.

To their surprise, the Indian population steadily increased. The BIA, instead of being able to work itself out of a job, has found itself faced with even greater responsibilities. The growing need in many Indian communities for health, education, and economic development programs has only intensified the involvement of the BIA in the day-to-day lives of Indian people.

In the future, the issues facing both the BIA and American Indians will continue to be complex. Indians and non-Indians will have to agree upon an acceptable definition of the legal relationship between the federal government and American Indians. In addition, Indian people, their leaders, and their political organizations must decide how they want the BIA to serve them. The means for solving most problems in American Indian communities already exist. Another reorganization of the BIA would probably have little effect.

Instead, American Indians need to educate Congress and the American public about international agreements that focus on the inherent rights of native peoples. There must be a strong public consensus among non-Indians that they will no longer tolerate the mistreatment of Indians.

The BIA needs to exist to carry out the federal government's trust responsibility, an obligation to preserve and protect what rightfully belongs to American Indians. As many Indian leaders have often and eloquently stated, the federal government has a responsibility to honor Indians' treaty rights *and* their human rights for as long as the sun shall shine, the mountains stand, the grass is green, and the rivers flow. If these promises are kept, there will be no need for a magic formula for the future in Indian affairs.

Bureau of Indian Affairs
DEPARTMENT OF THE INTERIOR

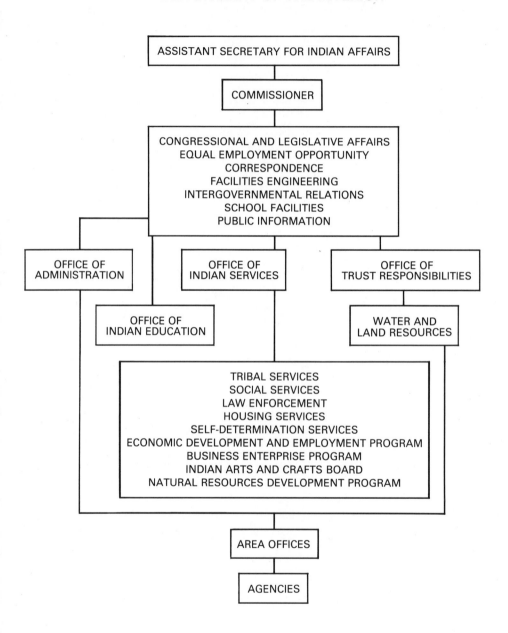

ASSISTANT SECRETARY FOR INDIAN AFFAIRS

COMMISSIONER

CONGRESSIONAL AND LEGISLATIVE AFFAIRS
EQUAL EMPLOYMENT OPPORTUNITY
CORRESPONDENCE
FACILITIES ENGINEERING
INTERGOVERNMENTAL RELATIONS
SCHOOL FACILITIES
PUBLIC INFORMATION

OFFICE OF
ADMINISTRATION

OFFICE OF
INDIAN SERVICES

OFFICE OF
TRUST RESPONSIBILITIES

OFFICE OF
INDIAN EDUCATION

WATER AND
LAND RESOURCES

TRIBAL SERVICES
SOCIAL SERVICES
LAW ENFORCEMENT
HOUSING SERVICES
SELF-DETERMINATION SERVICES
ECONOMIC DEVELOPMENT AND EMPLOYMENT PROGRAM
BUSINESS ENTERPRISE PROGRAM
INDIAN ARTS AND CRAFTS BOARD
NATURAL RESOURCES DEVELOPMENT PROGRAM

AREA OFFICES

AGENCIES

GLOSSARY

Agent A BIA official who lives among an Indian tribe and administers policy at the local level.

Allotment policy The Indian policy pursued by the federal government between 1887 and 1934. Under this policy, Indian reservations were carved into small plots of land that were distributed to individual Indians for the purpose of farming.

Annuity An annual payment made by the federal government to an Indian tribe according to the terms of a treaty or some other kind of official agreement.

Assimilation The complete absorption of one group into another group's cultural tradition.

"Civilization" policy A policy under which the U.S. government attempted to assimilate the Indians into the dominant society by teaching them European ways.

Peace commission Temporary bargaining team assembled by the president prior to a peace conference with Indians.

Pueblo An Indian dwelling built of adobe, a sun-dried building material made from earth and straw.

Reservation An area of land reserved by the federal government for use by Indians.

Self-determination The federal government's current Indian policy, which gives tribes freedom to choose whether or not to remain on reservations, whether or not to form tribal governments, and whether or not to assume responsibility for services traditionally provided by the BIA.

Trading house A frontier outpost at which government personnel provided Indians with commercially manufactured goods in exchange for furs. The Indian Department operated these outlets between 1796 and 1822 in an attempt to exert greater federal control over commerce with the Indians.

SELECTED REFERENCES

Deloria, Vine, Jr. *Behind the Trail of Broken Treaties*. New York: Dell, 1974.

Hagan, William T. *American Indians*. Chicago: University of Chicago Press, 1979.

Jackson, Curtis E., and Marcia J. Galli. *A History of the Bureau of Indian Affairs and Its Activities Among Indians*. San Francisco: R & R Research Associates, Inc., 1977.

Kvasnicka, Robert M., and Herman J. Viola, eds. *The Commissioners of Indian Affairs*. Lincoln: University of Nebraska Press, 1979.

Matthiessen, Peter. *In the Spirit of Crazy Horse*. New York: Viking Press, 1983.

Meriam, Lewis, et al. *The Problem of Indian Administration*. Institute for Government Research, Studies in Administration. Baltimore: Johns Hopkins University Press, 1928.

Philip, Kenneth R. *John Collier's Crusade for Indian Reform, 1920–1954*. Tucson: University of Arizona Press, 1977.

Prucha, Francis Paul. *American Indian Policy in Crisis: Christian Reformers and the Indian, 1865–1900*. Norman: University of Oklahoma Press, 1976.

―――. *American Indian Policy in the Formative Years: The Indian Trade and Intercourse Acts, 1790–1834*. Cambridge, MA: Harvard University Press, 1962.

Schmeckebeier, Laurence F. *The Office of Indian Affairs: Its History, Activities, and Organization*. Baltimore: Johns Hopkins University Press, 1927.

Steiner, Stan. *The New Indians*. New York: Harper & Row, 1968.

Stuart, Paul. *The Indian Office: Growth and Development of an American Institution, 1865–1900*. Ann Arbor: University of Michigan Press, 1979.

Szasz, Margaret. *Education and the American Indian: The Road to Self-Determination, 1928–1973*. Albuquerque: University of New Mexico Press, 1975.

Taylor, Theodore W. *American Indian Policy*. Mt. Airy, MD: Lomond Press, 1983.

―――. *The Bureau of Indian Affairs*. Boulder, Colorado: Westview Press, 1959.

INDEX

Frank W. Porter III, General Editor of INDIANS OF NORTH AMERICA, is Director of the Chelsea House Foundation for American Indian Studies. He holds an M.A. and Ph.D. in Ethnohistory from the University of Maryland, where he also earned his B.A., and he has done extensive research concerning the Indians of Maryland and Delaware. He was formerly Director of the Maryland Commission on Indian Affairs and the American Indian Research and Resource Institute, Gettysburg, Pennsylvania, and he has received grants from the Delaware Humanities Forum, the Maryland Committee for the Humanities, the Ford Foundation, and the National Endowment for the Humanities, among others. Dr. Porter is the author of *The Nanticoke* in the Chelsea House series INDIANS OF NORTH AMERICA.

Arthur M. Schlesinger, jr., served in the White House as special assistant to Presidents Kennedy and Johnson. He is the author of numerous acclaimed works in American history and has twice been awarded the Pulitzer Prize. He taught history at Harvard College for many years and is currently Albert Schweitzer Professor of the Humanities at the City College of New York.

PICTURE CREDITS: